"A must read! Like a bright shooting star ~~~~~~~~~~~~~~~~~~~~~~~~~~~~~~
Kumashiro persuasively describes how the broader Left often talks
about the 'problem' in outdated ways and offers a unique path forward
in the overlapping arenas of K–12 education and higher education."

—Clarence B. Jones,
former political advisor, personal lawyer, and
draft speechwriter to Rev. Dr. Martin Luther King Jr.

"Kevin Kumashiro's book comes at exactly the right moment in American history, as the nation debates how to rid itself of centuries of
racism. Kumashiro challenges the reader to rethink ingrained assumptions. He seeks to reframe the narratives in which those perceived as
'others' are deeply embedded. His book calls upon its readers to free
their minds from stale beliefs. It is enlightening and provocative."

—Diane Ravitch,
founder and president, Network for Public Education

"Like all good educators, Kevin Kumashiro knows that whether they
are teachers, administrators, teacher educators, or others who care
deeply about public education and the future of our democracy, all
educators must also of necessity be community educators and organizers who challenge business as usual. In this groundbreaking book,
Kumashiro provides a vision for the organizer in each of us as we work
toward a truly transformative education."

—Sonia Nieto,
professor emerita, University of Massachusetts Amherst

"Drawing upon his scholarship and lessons learned over the past 20
years, Kumashiro deftly provides a succinct history and radical reframing of the contentious issues in education today. Calling upon progressives to challenge the prevailing 'common sense' assumptions of
schooling, the move toward market-based reforms, and the narrow
focus on individual outcomes, he advances an alternative vision of
education as a collective investment and responsibility."

—Michael Omi,
professor, University of California, Berkeley

"If you don't know the brilliant work of Kevin Kumashiro on educa-tion, social justice, and equity, you couldn't find a better, more time-ly, and informative way to get acquainted with him than this book. Kumashiro is candid and blunt: education is about moral, illuminat-ing, and liberating ideas for the bodies and minds of all people, not just some people whose skin is White. The award-winning author ex-plains why progressives lose the biggest battles in education to rac-ism. Kumashiro's insights will prompt a great deal of head-nodding, and his suggestions to bring about social justice and equity are within the reach and power of all educators. To question and challenge, and to remake the common sense of this moment in order to create a social-justice world, is the educational journey Kumashiro wants you to take with him. Join him!"

—Carl A. Grant,
Hoefs Bascom Professor, University of Wisconsin–Madison

"*Surrendered* embodies problem-posing education at its best. Kevin Kumashiro, like other exemplary teachers and organizers, challenges us to shake off the burden of our fixed and calcified assumptions as we rethink first principles and fundamental issues: What would a sys-tem of schools look like in a more just and thoroughly participatory society? What would it mean to co-create with students and families a curriculum and an action plan to resist, rather than perpetuate, histor-ic injustices? What could schools become if we reimagined education, not as a sorting machine and a hypercompetitive rat race kids are re-quired to run, but as a dynamic site designed to respond to the dreams of both youth and communities? As he digs deeply into the history of social justice struggles in education, Kumashiro uncovers a disturbing reality: freedom fighters and justice seekers have repeatedly, if inad-vertently, surrendered to the Right by accepting preestablished terms of the struggle nested in the powerful, unyielding dogma of common sense—a quality shrewdly deployed by the guardians of the status quo. Kumashiro is an ideal guide for these times: curious and thought-ful, principled and agile, spirited and compassionate. He reminds us that there is no example of justice achieved without risk, courage, and disruption—and he beckons us to join him in that great work."

—William Ayers,
series editor, Teaching for Social Justice Series

Surrendered

Why Progressives Are Losing the Biggest Battles in Education

Kevin K. Kumashiro

TEACHERS COLLEGE PRESS

TEACHERS COLLEGE | COLUMBIA UNIVERSITY
NEW YORK AND LONDON

Published by Teachers College Press,® 1234 Amsterdam Avenue, New York, NY
10027

Library of Congress Control Number: 2020944762

ISBN 978-0-8077-6460-2 (paper)
ISBN 978-0-8077-6461-9 (hardcover)
ISBN 978-0-8077-7920-0 (ebook)

Printed on acid-free paper
Manufactured in the United States of America

To the casualties when Progressives surrender

Contents

Preface

This book headed to press in early summer 2020, just as uprisings began across the United States and the world to protest police killings of Black men, women, trans people, and children, and to challenge anti-Black racism more broadly. Some of the uprisings coincided with destruction of property. The media, leaders in both political parties, and some educators were quick to contrast the good actors—those who protested peacefully and followed the law—with the bad actors—labeled as looters, purposely causing damage, and not part of the sanctioned protests.

This simplistic and problematic framing of good-versus-bad reminded me of a teacher colleague who once told me that when students act out in ways that we might label bad, she would ask herself: What are they trying to tell me that they could not find a way to tell me before, or perhaps, were telling me but I was not able to hear until now? Her question echoed research spanning decades about historically marginalized populations of students acting out in schools, not because they were bad students or because they were unable to learn and succeed. No, they were acting out because, consciously or not, they were aware that schools were not working for them. Acting out was a form of resistance, of pushing back.

A similar argument has long been made about people rising up and acting against the United States, pushing back on our foreign policy and actions abroad that have caused untold levels of destruction, suffering, and oppression. However, because the general public was unaware of what our government and related sectors—like the military, financial institutions, and corporations—were doing, the blowback from abroad was misinterpreted as acts of evil, as terrorism, as attacks on us and on democracy itself.

Dr. Martin Luther King Jr., told us that "a riot is the language of the unheard," and with such a framing, he indicted not those who were pushing back, but that against which the masses were pushing. He indicted not those who were speaking out, but the state, which had refused to hear those whom it had for so long suppressed. Cornel West called the uprisings today a "reckoning," and we should be asking, are we indeed reckoning with what the uprisings are calling out?

The uprisings suggest to me three important questions for this moment, particularly as they concern education.

First, are we looking at the problem systemically? When we think of police murders of Black people, or other forms of police violence—as vividly captured in viral video recordings of police officers tackling, throwing to the ground, dragging, handcuffing, or macing Black children, or similar actions by the public, like the recent lynchings of Black men, that were followed by willful inaction by the state—and when we view such actions and we frame the problem as simply individuals-gone-bad—a bad police officer, a bad attorney—in an otherwise just system, we mask how the system was designed to function precisely as such. The criminal justice system is an instrument of the state, and as such, it works to maintain particular racial ideologies in the service of the state; it is itself a racial project.

This should sound familiar to those of us working in education, because the same can be said about education. Much of the rhetoric we hear in education blames teachers or students or parents, which reduces the problems in education to the actions of bad outliers in an otherwise good system. But as many of us have researched or personally experienced or observed, the reality is that educational systems are also instruments of the state and, as with policing and incarceration, were designed to function with disparate outcomes. Rhetoric would have us believe that education is meant to provide equal educational opportunity, but from the inception of education in this country, schools were not designed to serve everyone. Over time, as schooling became available to the masses, schools came up with different ways to differentiate and sort through exclusion, tracking, labeling, discipline, and of course, through curriculum, through what and how we teach. Some students and communities are acutely aware that this is and has always been happening, effectively so and by design. What would it mean to reckon with this fact?

Second, are we looking at the problem intersectionally, and if so, are we connecting the dots? The United States—its identity, its economy, its culture—was founded on slavery. It was also founded on the theft, colonization, and genocide of Indigenous peoples. It was also founded on heteropatriarchal ideologies, including how we conceptualize and regulate public-versus-private spheres, family, relationships, and love itself. It was an Imperialist project even before its founding, and continues to be so now. It has so embraced Neoliberalism as to make unquestioned its normalcy as the operative ideology in any number of sectors, from the economy to healthcare to education. And all of these forces and legacies intersect to both reinforce and be reinforced by anti-blackness; this is why some of the most generative social movements today—Black Lives

Matter, Green New Deal—are intentionally intersectional. Educational movements must be so as well.

Third, are we looking at what the role of education is in this moment? Over the last few months, I have seen several excellent webinars on what educators can do: ways to teach, to speak out, to comfort those who struggle with trauma and grief and loss, to care for ourselves. These are important. But we should be cautious not to reinforce narratives of effective or impactful teaching as only that which happens by one person. Education is impoverished when treated hyper-individualistically.

As educators, scholars, leaders, or advocates, we must find more ways to act collectively to make good on the promise of education in and for a democracy. I remember when I was starting out as a teacher, and some of us would speak longingly of the time in the near future when we were secure enough in our jobs as to be able to close the classroom door and do brilliant things in our rooms, unencumbered by the latest reforms and pressures on teachers that have hindered the ability to teach. Then and now, such pressures are indeed problems, but the solution should not be to retreat to isolation; our work in education is weakened when we do it on our own, without a critical mass of collaborators to help us imagine, plan, create, practice, assess, advocate, and transform.

More broadly, educational institutions must find more ways to act in solidarity with the communities around us. In the midst of crises, like what we find ourselves in today with projections of education budgets being slashed, the tendency is to shrink, to cut back, to do less as a way to spend less. Educational institutions have long been criticized for being disconnected from communities and irrelevant to their needs and challenges, and some of us would therefore insist that, by stepping back in the midst of historic levels of suffering, unemployment, illness, violence, anxiety, and uprising, we make ourselves even more disconnected, more irrelevant, more inconsequential, and more complacent. We need to find more ways to step up, ways of collaborating with the many facets of the community—the public sector, the private sector, unions, community-based organizations, families, faith groups, artists, activists, the media—to better serve and build the capacity of the community, as best illustrated by "community schools" that are expanding, troubling, and transforming how we understand the very purpose and the very nature of educational institutions. What can and should be the intervention of education in this moment, or in any moment?

I can think of no better way to open this book than with these questions as guides to writing and reading what follows and with the uprisings as our call to action.

Acknowledgments

This book draws on many essays, presentations, media interviews, and conversations that I have contributed to over the past few years, and I wish to thank all who invited, sparked, supported, challenged, or simply accompanied me towards and through this work, including comrades at forums and colleges around the world, the Underground University, EDJE, CReATE, CARE-ED, HSESJ, teacher activist groups and unions, Insight Into Diversity, Institute for Public Accuracy, public-radio and public-access television programs and stations, and participants of my past conferences and workshops.

Thank you to Ruchi Agarwal-Rangnath, Rick Ayers, Stacey Lee, and especially Carol Batker, four of my dearest friends, for sharing generously your vision, insights, encouragement, and exquisite attention to detail that clarified for me the intervention that this book, or portions of, could and should aim to make in this moment, and how to do so.

Thank you to Brian Ellerbeck for supporting and shepherding this project with much care, and to the staff, reviewers, editors, and everyone at Teachers College Press for the countless aspects of making this book possible in such challenging times.

Thank you to Carl Grant, Clarence Jones, Sonia Nieto, Michael Omi, and Diane Ravitch—each of whom have guided and inspired me for decades—for so generously providing the beautiful endorsements.

Thank you especially to Bill Ayers for helping me to envision this project over 3 years ago, and in the time since, for providing the most brilliant and helpful guidance ever on drafts (and life, in general), and for accepting this book into this most wonderful book series.

And thank you to all those before and around me on whose Progressive visions and labors I aspire to build.

Surrendered

Introduction

NAMING THE MOMENT

As I write this book in spring 2020, the world is already (only?) a few months into the COVID-19 pandemic. Much can happen in a time of crisis.

A crisis can bring out the best in us. As our country shelters in place and shutters schools, news and social media are being flooded with touching stories of teachers going the extra mile to offer enriching curriculum, comforting words, and ongoing contact—sometimes through email, phone, websites, and video conferencing, and sometimes simply by driving through their students' neighborhoods to wave, greet, and remind one another that their lives still intersect.

In a refreshing counter to years of rhetoric and policy that blamed, demonized, and punished teachers, social media amplifies the gratitude and praise by parents—now struggling to support at-home learning—for teachers and the vast knowledge, skills, flexibility, and compassion those teachers bring to their children's learning and healthy growth. A crisis can help to expose what is often taken for granted, not only about teachers, but also about all that schools offer: supervised spaces and enrichment activities; a refuge for students for whom the home is not safe, or who have no home to go to; meals and nutrition for tens of millions of students; and vital medical and mental-health services to students who may not be able to access them otherwise. Without school-based medical care, some students have no easy options, as illustrated by a California teenager who died after being turned away from an urgent-care facility, while showing symptoms of COVID-19, because of lack of health insurance.

In the midst of a crisis, as stress and anxiety mount, it is easy to ask the wrong questions and to direct frustration and anger at the wrong target. As most schools across the country close and students are expected to study at home, complaints abound on social media about homework. Upset about the volume of homework, and as schools and teachers face pressure to stay on pace and not fall behind, some students and parents ask, "Why so many worksheets?" Upset about the content of the homework, students are asking, "How am I supposed to learn all of this?" and parents asking, "How am I supposed to help my children learn this?" as they struggle to cover new material without a teacher.

The frustration builds on anxieties about what is missed out on and how that can impact their future. Will students learn everything that they were supposed to learn this year, or will that content be covered in the summer or fall, for those who are not graduating this spring? Will they be ready for the mountains of testing that normally happens in the spring, which some argue should not be cancelled, simply postponed to the fall? Will schools even reopen in the fall for in-person learning? Will they be less prepared for college, or their future career, or life in general, because they received less materials and failed to meet standards? And how are all of these worksheets supposed to accomplish that?

The anxiety is understandable, given the stories that circulate from political leaders, the media, employers, and even schools, about how important those standards, and those tests, and all those materials are to succeed educationally and economically. But the tendency to focus narrowly on individuals and blame one another—for not being realistic, for not communicating well, for not staying motivated and disciplined— can detract from the broken systems in which individuals operate. Rather than wondering how to stay on pace, a more fundamental question might be: Are efforts to stay on pace replicating some of the most problematic aspects of schools, like contested standards, irrelevant or test-driven or dumbed-down curriculum, over-testing, mountains of homework and worksheets, expectations to teach yourself, resource inequities between schools, between homes, between the haves and the have-nots? *Yes, a crisis can bring out the best in us, but when we fail to ask the right questions, it can also reveal or amplify the worst, and in a number of ways, this is precisely what is happening with the COVID-19 crisis.*

Racialized Disease

Accused of carrying the COVID-19, a Chinese American student in California was beaten so badly by peers that he needed to be hospitalized. This was February 2020, in the early weeks of the pandemic, when reports were already surfacing of increased levels of harassment, violence, threats, and discrimination against Asians and Asian Americans. President Donald Trump and other leaders and media personalities continued to use terms like "Chinese virus" and "kung flu," and defended doing so, despite widespread condemnation of such terms as misleading and inflammatory. In mid-March, the Stop AAPI Hate website recorded over 650 incidents of race-based attacks across the country—verbal and physical, in and outside of schools—in just its first week of operation.

Whether about teasing, attacking, ostracizing, or refusing services, stories of harassment and discrimination commonly revolved around an underlying fear that "the Chinese" are more likely to be the ones carrying and spreading the disease. Given that some people cannot or do not differentiate between Asian ethnic groups, and given the stereotype that people of Asian descent are all foreigners in the United States, it is not surprising that many of the targets of attack included Chinese Americans who had not recently or ever been in China, as well as Asian Americans of other ethnic backgrounds.

Associating disease with a particular country or race has social and policy consequences. From the early 1800s to early 1900s, Chinese (and, at times, Japanese) immigrants were blamed for spreading bubonic plague, cholera, smallpox, syphilis, trachoma, and even sexual deviance, resulting in school segregation, systematic destruction of homes and property, and immigration restrictions.

In 2003, anti-Asian attacks again increased during the SARS pandemic. Today, some leaders misrepresent history in order to perpetuate this racializing of disease, as when one Republican senator, while defending Trump's terminology, blamed the Chinese for the swine flu and MERS, despite the fact that neither originated in China. Even the 1918–1919 influenza pandemic, often erroneously called the Spanish Flu pandemic, has been blamed by some people on China, despite the lack of consensus among researchers about its origins.

At times, the racialization of disease has derived from perceived cultural deficits, such as living in filthy homes and eating unusual animals. But increasingly throughout the 20th century, the fear of racialized diseases spreading in and debilitating the United States has constituted part of a larger narrative of the Yellow Peril, a centuries-old stereotype that Asia and Asians pose a threat of invasion and conquest, which could come in any number of forms. In the 1940s, fears of military invasion and conquest during World War II contributed to the incarceration of 120,000 Japanese Americans. In the 1980s, the growth of the Japanese economy prompted fears of economic invasion and conquest that instigated not only trade barriers, but also hatred and violence, as when hatred toward Japanese competitors in the auto industry translated to hate crimes against Asian Americans more broadly, including the murder of Vincent Chin. Post-9/11, fears of a religious war fueled hate crimes, racial profiling, and extralegal incarceration of Muslims and those perceived to be Muslim, including South Asians and Middle Easterners. In recent years, some in universities fear the academic invasion and conquest by "too many" Chinese international students.

In the midst of today's pandemic, reflected in any number of emails and postings on social media that are replete with inaccuracies but nonetheless going viral, is a fear that China is engaging in germ warfare, intentionally spreading the virus to weaken the economies of other countries, particularly the United States. According to this conspiracy theory, the Chinese are not merely diseased, but also have weaponized disease, for how else could China have built a hospital and mobilized tens of thousands of medical professionals so quickly, or contained the spread and lifted aspects of lockdown so quickly; how else could China's economy have survived the stock market crash in early 2020 that leveled so many other countries, had they not planned for it beforehand?

Inflaming anxieties about a new Yellow Peril detracts from critical analysis of what is actually happening here and now. Instead, Americans need to be asking why the United States is not nationalizing its healthcare system, as others have already done, in order to marshal its vast resources and make medical care more widely available; or why the United States is not using the Defense Production Act, which it does all the time for other purposes, to redirect industries to serve this crisis by creating more of the equipment so desperately needed; or why the richest country in the world, months into this crisis, still has not developed the capacity for adequate and widespread testing, contact tracing, isolation, and other public-health interventions; or, for that matter, why the federal government continues to respond with unprecedented levels of corporate bailouts and deregulation that exacerbate the conditions of inequity that have made it so difficult for the United States to respond to this crisis effectively in the first place.

Stereotypes arise, persist, and re-emerge at particular moments because they serve political purposes. Attacking China and people of Asian descent by conjuring the long histories of racialized disease and Yellow Peril serves effectively to detract attention from the failures of the Trump administration to address today's pandemic, as well as the failures of previous administrations and Congresses to fix the broken systems that are made all the more apparent in this time of crisis. The U.S. economy, after all, was a bloated bubble ready to burst, inflated by policies that have been obscured by the distraction of crises, which of course is the point—to obscure how we got here so that the solution can be more of the same.

Following the 2008–2009 mortgage crisis, the federal government gifted trillions of dollars in corporate bailouts, claiming that such assistance would trickle down to the middle and working classes. But such a trickle did not happen. Instead, Congress further deregulated financial institutions and corporations, failing to hold them accountable for irresponsibility and greed, such as insufficient insurance and buffers and exorbitant salaries, rewards, and perks to the leaders and investors alongside unlivable incomes for the working masses, respectively. This, in effect, incentivized more irresponsibility, greed, inflation, and risk. A new bubble would grow, bigger than before, creating a wealth gap—between the poor, in historically large numbers, and the rich, with unprecedented concentrated wealth—that would become even larger than the gap that existed just before the Great Depression. When the market crashed in early 2020, the federal response was more of the same: so-called stimulus packages, larger than any before, that sent insufficiently little to struggling individuals and households while lavishing far more onto corporations and the elite.

The United States has a long history of taking advantage of—and, at times, even stoking—crises and disasters to transform public policies to benefit corporations and the elite. An exemplar of this happening in the field of education can be found in the plan to rebuild New Orleans post-Katrina, a precursor to what is happening today.

Corona-Capitalism

In 2010, then-Secretary of Education Arne Duncan proclaimed that Hurricane Katrina in 2005 was the "best thing that happened to the education system" of New Orleans. The flooding and destruction that forced the citywide closure of schools provided an opportunity for a state takeover, ostensibly to improve a district that, according to Duncan, was a "disaster." The blueprint for this takeover was part of a larger set of proposals by the Republican Study Committee—the congressional caucus that drives Conservative legislation, chaired by current vice president Mike Pence—for leveraging the natural disaster to advance pro-free-market reforms.

The committee's education proposals centered on privatizing education and diverting public funds by expanding school choice. Federal vouchers came right away through the 2005 Katrina Emergency Relief Act, followed by state vouchers in 2012 in the form of the Louisiana Scholarship Program, which today sends an overwhelming majority of students to the lowest performing private schools. Nationwide, vouchers do not necessarily help low-income students or students of color to attend higher performing schools, and in some states, they are in the minority of those using vouchers.

As New Orleans schools reopened, almost all were transformed into charters. The district became even more racially segregated than before Katrina. The charters serving poorer Black students commonly fired veteran Black teachers from the community and hired Teach for America teachers with short-term contracts, who constituted the majority of the instructional staff in some schools. Nationwide, charter schools show significantly higher rates of teacher turnover; they serve fewer students with disabilities and English-language learners; some states, like Texas, pay far more per pupil at charters than traditional public schools; and the federal government has wasted hundreds of millions of dollars on grants to charters that either went defunct soon after or were never opened.

Pro-free-market reforms continue to define the agenda of the billionaires, mega-philanthropies, and corporations that exert unrivalled influence over education, particularly for poorer communities of color. Examples of some of the biggest or most influential funders include the Laura and John Arnold Foundation, Bloomberg Philanthropies, the Lynde and Harry Bradley Foundation, the Eli and Edyth Broad Foundation, the Chan Zuckerberg Initiative, the City Fund, the DeVos family foundations, the Bill and Melinda Gates Foundation, the Koch family foundations, and the Walton Family Foundation. Whether the funders and advocates lean Conservative, as most do, or Liberal, Republican or Democrat (see, for example, the platform of Democrats for Education Reform), their priorities converge into the portfolio model of reform, now spreading to urban districts across the United States. This model decentralizes decision-making, expands school choice, holds schools accountable through performance measures like student testing, and sanctions failing schools with restructuring or closure, incentivizing their replacements in the form of charter schools.

As the COVID-19 crisis unfolds, proponents of market-based reforms have wasted little time capitalizing on the same two conditions that propelled privatization post-Katrina—school closures and emergency federal funding—except at a scale without precedent. Some states, including Ohio and Tennessee, have pushed to expand or accelerate voucher programs, and Secretary of Education Betsy DeVos has proposed a new way to advance vouchers as microgrants. Federal stimulus funding provided hundreds of billions of dollars for small businesses, some of which went to charter schools.

Stimulus funding as of March 2020 also included over $13 billion directly to states and districts for K–12 education, but provided much leeway in how they spent that. As schools struggled with the sudden need to provide distance or remote instruction, much of those funds were likely to be spent on educational technology, which included not only computers and internet access, but also online schools, resources, and related services.

Technology can enhance education, but the misuse of or overreliance on technology can exacerbate existing resource inequities between schools and between homes, particularly for students in poverty, homeless students, and students with disabilities. Other concerns include data privacy, online bullying, sexual exploitation, and the negative impact of extensive screen time on literacy development, mental health, and physical health.

Across the country, some of the closed schools were not providing institutional support for instruction. In Los Angeles alone, tens of thousands of students were either not regularly checking in online, or not checking in at all. School achievement—test scores, grades—and attainment, such as graduation and postsecondary education, go down when students miss a significant amount of school. The educational gap between working-class and middle-class students widens over summer break, because far more educational opportunities are available to middle-class students. Heavy reliance on homework also widens gaps between families in which parents have different levels of education, as parents with higher levels of education are better able to assist with homework. Low-income and disinvested neighborhoods are more likely to expose students to higher levels of violence, homelessness, emotional stress, physical-health hazards such as pollutants and toxins, anxieties about financial security, and interpersonal tensions within households as economic conditions worsen—all with compounding effects when students are sheltering at home and kept out of schools for periods far longer than normal.

For years, a constellation of Liberals, Conservatives, and technology-related funding organizations—such as Laurene Powell Jobs, Rupert Murdoch, and Amplify, respectively—have pushed for a vision of education that centers on technology as a primary lever for change, not merely to enhance curriculum, but to be the primary source of or platform for curriculum and instruction. With so much federal stimulus funding at stake, and schools relying on technology to continue education, there could not be a better time to push forward this vision to technologize, privatize, and profiteer, despite the negative consequences.

In April 2020, over 550 educators and scholars of color from across the United States joined me in issuing a statement, "This Must End Now: Educators and Scholars of Color Against Failed Educational 'Reforms,'" calling for a retreat from the market-based, so-called reforms being foisted by billionaires upon poorer communities of color. Such initiatives have not systematically improved student success, are faulty by design, and have already proven to widen racial and economic disparities. There are better alternatives. As the United States struggles to address the current pandemic, communities must not be seduced by the pro-free-market ideologies that brought schools to this point in the first place.

Lessons from 1919

Much can be learned from the 1918–1919 flu pandemic. That was the first time that the United States saw school closures nationwide, some for months. There was no vaccine; the first large-scale use of a vaccine would not occur until 1945. Students and many adults stayed at home, and not surprisingly, within families and households where someone was ill, infections spread. Given that poorer families were more likely in crowded housing conditions; more likely to continue working in jobs with high exposure to others, such as the industrial, consumer, and service sectors; and least likely to have easy access to medical care, they were the hardest hit.

These were exactly the conditions that fueled the spread of COVID-19 in Wuhan in the first few weeks of the lockdown in early 2020. In Wuhan, and subsequently in other East Asian countries like South Korea and Taiwan, it was not merely the modifying of individual behavior, like quarantining at home, that would slow the spread, but additionally, the public-health initiatives of testing, contact tracing, and isolation, alongside medical treatment. Quarantining is necessary but insufficient, and as millions of U.S. school children shelter at home without adequate public-health and medical intervention, we can similarly expect the hardest hit to be the ones made most vulnerable by poverty.

But the story of the 1918–1919 pandemic does not end with the outbreak itself. In 1919, as the pandemic was ending, and still reeling from post–World War I wage freezes, Seattle saw a general strike where workers not only fought for better working conditions, but did so as they worked to create the society that they aspired towards: while striking, they were also providing social services and resources to the poor.

In the early months of the COVID-19 pandemic in the United States, strikes and work stoppages happened in several states as workers pushed back on employers who prioritized profit over their workers. Unions nationwide had been more frequently debating what it would mean for them to engage in "collective bargaining for the common good," as with the Chicago Teachers Union, whose 2019 strike, as well as its precedent-setting strike of 2012, provided a template of bargaining for the conditions that make possible quality public education, not for wages and compensation alone. Other collectives beyond unions had been recently striking as well: teachers in right-to-work states in 2018 who engaged in wildcat strikes or walkouts, gaining increased funding for public schools, and youth actions like climate strikes and walkouts for safety and gun control among the most notable examples.

How will schools—and U.S. society, and the world—emerge from our current crisis? A crisis is a moment of both frantic energy and disquieting pause; it offers an opportunity to fundamentally transform, in good and in bad ways, with various stakeholders struggling and competing to shape that path forward. What gives any reform an edge in this struggle is the extent to which it builds on ideas already in the mainstream about what could and should be the way forward. *Therefore, how the United States emerges from this crisis will have everything to do with the "common sense" of our times.*

QUESTIONING COMMON SENSE

I needed a time out. About 30 years ago, it was a gorgeous Hawai'i summer during morning recess when I saw one of my rascally preschool students swinging on a low-hanging branch in the playground. Before I could warn him to stop, I was distracted by I-do-not-remember-what, and by the time I turned back, he had managed to rip off the branch and, though by himself, wield it like a sword against, perhaps, imaginary demons. Time for a time out! It is just common sense that we do not break apart our trees to use as toys, right? At nap time that afternoon, I did my rounds to check in on each student, and when I knelt down beside him, he asked me if he was bad today, with a sincerity that made me pause. Perhaps my rule was not so commonsensical, at least, not to him.

The use of what may be considered to be common sense to discipline has given me pause on any number of occasions. A parent once told me of her son at his first and only summer construction job, who early on was tasked with sawing off a metal rod that was protruding from a concrete block. After guessing that the saw would more easily cut through concrete than metal, he attempted to saw through the middle of the block at a point beyond where the metal was presumably inserted. The foreman asked the mother what was wrong with her son, and why he did not have enough common sense to just cut the thin metal rather than the thick concrete, to which the mother replied that it might have been common sense to the foreman, but it was not common sense to everyone; it was obviously not to her son, who had never worked construction before, nor would it have been to her, someone he had better not dare say lacked sense.

Common sense is not something that just is. No, common sense is something that evolves for a specific group of people, which means that it varies from place to place and alters over time. It is not the only way to think: It is a partial, incomplete, evolving story, but one that has consequence as it teaches, socializes, frames, negates, honors, and disciplines. What counts as common sense is often what stabilizes the status quo, or at least enables us to navigate that status quo, and, in so doing, preserves the privileges therein. Common sense cannot help but to be political, to be implicated in the injustices of our times, and thus, common sense can become intolerant, dogmatic, and insistent, especially when leveraged strategically for oppressive ends. *To frame common sense is to convince the masses to buy into a specific story of what and how the world is and must be.*

"It's Just Common Sense" headlined the full-page ad in the local newspaper from my hometown of Honolulu. It was the fall of 1998, only weeks before the general election, and on the ballot was a referendum to amend the state constitution to give the state legislature the authority to prohibit same-sex marriage. The referendum was meant to preempt the Hawai'i State Supreme Court, which was expected to rule at any moment that there was no compelling state interest to prohibit same-sex marriage. Hawai'i was poised to be the first state in the country to pass such legislation, garnering much attention, funding, and campaign resources for a battle that could and would set a precedent and a model for other states. "It's just common sense" that marriage is between a man and a woman, and therefore, that everyone should support the referendum, or so the thinking went. The referendum passed by over 60%, the state legislature quickly amended the state constitution to prohibit same-sex marriage, and as predicted, dozens of other states followed suit.

Common Sense in Education

When framed as common sense, whether or not backed by research, a reform is more likely to be supported, just as reforms that run counter to what is framed as common sense are more likely to be opposed. This is exactly what has been happening with educational reform since the creation of large public school systems in the early 20th century with various educational reform initiatives. If people believe it to be commonsensical that the school year should run from September to June, and someone comes along and proposes year-round schooling, that person faces an uphill battle. If it is believed to be commonsensical that the school day should run from 8:00 A.M. to 3:00 P.M.; or that schools should teach 50 minutes of math, 50 minutes of reading, and 50 minutes of other subjects daily or weekly; or that students should be grouped in certain ways—by age, by ability, by race—and along comes someone who proposes a change, that person faces an uphill battle.

The difficulty in changing the status quo is not because the research backs up the common sense; there is no compelling body of research that says that schools are most effective if organized in these ways, nor have schools always been organized in these ways, in this country or around the world. No, what materializes as the common sense of schools are historical products, having emerged at particular moments for particular reasons—shaped by things like the workforce calendar of a preindustrial society, or the organizing principles of large factories, or the proposals of influential foundations and leaders—which then persist because they become the standard of how schools should be.

A hundred years ago, it was commonsensical in mainstream discourse to say that girls should not get too much education, and indeed, girls either did not go to school or went to school until only around the fifth grade. Why? Some people believed that women belonged in the home. Some people believed that women would compete with men for jobs. Some believed what was passing for science at the time that the mind was connected to the body, that distorting up one might distort the other, and therefore, that if girls got too much education, they might become insane, physically ill, or even infertile. Today, such views about women's roles and female bodies might sound outdated or unsubstantiated, but at the time, for some people, such views went unquestioned.

Fifty years ago, it was commonsensical in the dominant group and among the powerful to say that the descendants of enslaved workers, migrants from the global south, and Indigenous people should not get too much education, and indeed, communities nationwide fought to maintain separate, segregated, inferior schools for students of color, along with barriers for them to access higher education. Why? Some people believed that there would be competition for jobs. Some people believed what was passing for science at the time that people of darker skin were not as smart, and that schools should not waste time and resources teaching them. Many people today look back and think, "what a racist idea!" but for many people then, and even for some today, that idea went unquestioned, and it shaped policy and practice.

These histories raise the question, "How might people look back 50 or 100 years from now and say, 'I cannot believe that, in 2020, it was commonsensical to think this'?" What is the common sense of today that people are not even recognizing as perverse, as distorted pictures of reality, as misguided strategies? Why does the curriculum in many schools today look similar to the curriculum in schools decades ago, despite the fact that for decades, scholars have critiqued such curriculum as insufficient, ungrounded in research, and antidemocratic? Why do both political parties support high-stakes testing, despite the ample statistical evidence that such measures are neither valid nor reliable for the decisionmaking that results? Why does our society treat education as a commodity, whereby those who have the resources can buy better schooling, resulting in the "haves" having even more?

The challenge here is not merely to question the common sense about education, but more fundamentally, to question common sense through education. Education should not serve to assimilate minds into the common sense of the times, which is why so much of standards-based reform misses the boat as it demands that students think in ways that those in power want them to think.

In a Totalitarian state, education would serve presumably to conform minds, to get people to buy into the stories of or by those in power with the intention that the masses would then unquestioningly follow their lead. The correspondingly apartheid schooling system would likely consist of a few well-resourced, high-standards schools for the elite, and many more dehumanizing, under-resourced, dumbed-down schools for the masses—which is a system that sounds frighteningly and precisely like what exists here in the United States today. Some people presume, or even insist, that the U.S. educational system is democratic, or that it serves democracy, but the reality is far more complex and contested, thus raising the question: What can and should be the difference between education that serves inequity and Totalitarianism versus education for free people in a democracy?

In a democracy, education should aim not only to prepare students in the wide range of literacies that constitute the world as it is, but also to challenge and nourish their individual and collective capacities to imagine and create the world that is not yet, the world as it could or should be, and if they so choose, to build the tools to change all that is before them. To do so, education would need to involve questioning, rattling, challenging, and at times, remaking the common sense of our times, not conforming to it, or authorizing it, or normalizing it. Education should be about inquiry, imagination, liberation, transformation, democratization, and revolution, and that is why education—when done in the service of justice, and when treated as the vibrant site of political struggle that it is—can be seen by some, especially those in power, as scary and dangerous.

Questioning common sense is never easy. Even Progressives who are skilled at critiquing the injustices of a system can fall prey to commonsensical ideas that hinder any deep understanding of the problems and the solutions. The bipartisan support for market-based, "portfolio model" types of reforms in the midst of the COVID-19 crisis is one example. So, too, are any number of instances when Progressives claim progress and success. *Indeed, it is perhaps in spaces of supposed progress and success that common sense can be most insidious, most normative.*

Troubling Progress and Success

To say that education is about troubling common sense is to frame education, at its core, as an intervention *to queer*, to rattle the assimilative force of normalcy. Such is the intervention animated in the queer activism of the 1980s in the United States that shepherded one of the most significant reframings by any modern social movement.

Back in the early 1900s, deviations from normative sexualities and genders in the form of same-sex attraction, activity, and relationships, as well as transgender identity and transgressive gender presentations, were generally viewed and treated as a sin, an illness, or a crime. This common sense about sexual orientation and gender identity and expression impacted any number of arenas legally, medically, socially, culturally, religiously, economically, and psychologically by erecting boundaries of what and who counts as natural and normal, and by waging various technologies—criminalization, legal discrimination, medical procedures, conversation therapy, excommunication, negative media portrayals, social ostracism, physical violence—to ensure the exclusion of lesbian, gay, bisexual, transgender, questioning, intersex, asexual, two-spirit, and other non-heterosexual, non-normatively gendered, queer individuals (LGBTQIA+) from that prescribed norm.

In the mid-1900s, particularly the 1950s to 1970s, an LGBTQIA+ social movement would run tandem to the Civil Rights Movement and other social movements of that era, countering institutional attacks such as criminalization and medicalization, as well as social and moral attacks—from religious institutions, the mass media, and culture, as well as from individuals and groups—by challenging the commonsensical story that LGBTQIA+ were not normal and that there was something biologically, morally, psychologically wrong with them. Pro-rights marches and rallies would intentionally present men in business suits and women in dresses; community outreach would encourage coming out as LGBTQIA+; and lobbying initiatives would insist that LGBTQIA+ were everywhere, in families, workplaces, and circles of friends and neighbors, whether or not they were known as such. By demanding that they were as normal as everyone else, activists were pushing to expand the definition of normalcy in order for more LGBTQIA+ to fit in, to be included, whether that inclusion was for legal protection from discrimination or simply for social acceptance, which meant that, at least in part, this was a conformist strategy, an insistence that the collective *we* are just like *you*.

The queer activism of the 1980s departed from this messaging by insisting instead—through the spectacle and halting performance of flamboyant costumes and street theater that were intentionally and undeniably abnormal—that they did not want to be as normal as everyone else because there was something wrong with prevailing definitions of normalcy. Non-normative sexuality and gender became antinormative, a claiming of queerness as a standpoint from which to question, a political identity around which to collectivize and refuse the demand to conform by insisting that society trouble its notions of what and how sexuality, gender, and sex should be.

Throughout these decades of activism, there were unquestionably a number of significant gains in legal, medical, cultural, and various other arenas. Less clear, however, is the extent to which these changes served to queer. Narratives of "making progress" can fail to recognize how newer, seemingly less potent forms of discrimination can nonetheless be oppressive with as much or even more force than before, but insidiously so, as when expanding individual rights, but in ways that reinforce the normalcy or acceptability or even desirability of the institutions now righted to LGBTQIA+ people.

The biggest battles post-1980s included the right to serve in the military and the right to marry someone of the same gender. Although these struggles led to both cultural and economic gains—recognition, dignity; employment, financial benefits and entitlements—they nonetheless hinged on complicity with an Imperialist war industry, as well as on conformity with a heteropatriarchal institution of marriage. The post-1980s struggles over the military and marriage were about increasing the right to access mainstream institutions, to be treated like everyone else, but were not fundamentally about queering those institutions or the narratives on which they centered. The progress made was contradictory.

The act of queering progress is not unlike queering success. As with queer activism's troubling of normalcy, a queer standpoint invites the troubling of success and, in particular, the questioning of whether prevailing notions of success might be hegemonic; ideological tools that convince the masses to seek that which is quite oppressive. Failure might be standpoints from which to question the demand to conform that is se-ductively embodied in mainstream definitions of success. *Success, even and especially in making progress toward justice, demands a paradoxical undo-ing of itself, a discomforting inquiry into just how and how much so-called progress and success functioned to fuel broader systemic injustice.*

This has certainly been the contested terrain among queer activists in the two-sided successes of inclusion in the military and legal marriage, which is also apparent in struggles over education. If, for example, the purpose of schools is to socialize, to control, to conform, then success in schools is less about intelligence and growth, and more about being suc-cessfully conformed to dominant narratives of who an individual is and should be. Conversely, failure in school might be less a reflection of how smart, talented, hard-working, creative, or productive a student was, and more a consequence of schools needing many students to fail.

In contrast to viewing the categories of good or bad, of successful or failing as objective, as uncontested, and as prediscursive, the queering of those very binaries demands that schools recognize their socially con-structed, ideologically servicing nature as fragile and contingent, but po-litically significant—hence the deep investment in policing, reinforcing, and reproducing these categories.

It was never the case that a lot of students just happened to fail, or that students were failing on their own and schools just labeled them as such after the fact. No, it was always the case that reifying the successful student—and, for that matter, the effective school—required the contin-ued re-creation of a whole bunch of failing students to serve as the con-trast to success, which means that the failed student is constituted as such only through schooling. Schools narrowly define what it means to be a good student and then make all others into bad ones, as when saying that being a good student means sitting still for 45 minutes while listening to a lecture, which many cannot or will not always do; this in turn means that they then get labeled as disrespectful, or disruptive, or unstable, or attention-deficit, or disabled, or a troublemaker, or incapable of learning, which in turn can lead to being punished, kicked out, failed, or medicated.

Trying to uphold the narrow definition of good requires that schools proliferate the many ways of being bad. To serve its primary purpose of sorting, schools need to push some up and push all others down. One sign of just how controlled a people have become is the extent to which they either fight to be included in the push up, or they fight to prevent all others from joining them at the top, since both groups of fighters have bought into the story that everyone should want to achieve the narrow definition of success.

Like the struggles over the military and marriage, there are a number of Progressive struggles in education that ultimately and insidiously center on expanding access to and assimilating into problematic institutions, rather than queering those institutions. What would it mean for education to reframe common sense, to rattle its own norms, and in so doing, to queer?

THIS BOOK

Even before COVID-19, recent events in the United States had shined a national spotlight onto any number of issues in public education and elevated various policy and reform initiatives to the level of public debate, from Trump's pick in 2017 of billionaire school-choice proponent Betsy DeVos to be his Secretary of Education to the spring 2018 teacher wildcat strikes in six right-to-work states to the 2019 court case against Harvard's affirmative action admissions policy to the proposals by Democratic presidential hopefuls in 2019 to forgive student debt.

On these and other issues, Progressives have often found themselves stuck in the Conservative framings of issues that have endured over time, and not only failed to offer a radically different vision, but at key times in history, actively retreated from such a promise.

This book highlights how the broader Left—Progressives, Liberals, Democrats, teacher unions, civil-rights organizations—are often talking about the problem, in regard to education, in ways that were framed decades or even centuries ago by forces quite counter to the goals of democracy and justice, and in so doing, advancing supposed solutions that cannot help but to be counterproductive. This book explains when, why, and how that has happened, particularly regarding the biggest battles in public education today and the insidious nature of popular reforms—which are often reforms in name alone—and offers a different path forward in the overlapping arenas of K–12 education and higher education.

Part I presents a brief history of the forces that have shaped public education, including the legacies of Imperialism, White supremacy, Nationalism, Colonialism, the Cold War, unionizing, the Civil Rights Movement, Conservatism, and Neoliberalism, to name a few, as well as key moments when the retreat of the Left and of the federal government opened up space for a bipartisan convergence in Conservative terrain, illustrated by battles over privatization, school choice, and vouchers. Understanding what is happening in public education today, including the many initiatives to reform or transform schools, requires understanding how we got here, the goals and intentions of competing leaders and reformers, the intersection of education with a range of other social and political institutions, and the reverberations of the achievements and failures, compromises and convergences in these struggles. Such historicizing is particularly important for Progressives who wish to avoid a repetition of past surrenders.

Part II dives into more of the biggest battles in education today—affirmative action, free speech and hate speech, bullying and violence, teacher shortages, and student debt—by examining enduring frames and exploring alternative ones. Without new frames, Progressives are likely to continue offering reforms that may echo lofty rhetoric but serve to perpetuate the status quo, or that may address one aspect of the problem, but in ways that reinforce the larger whole. The intersectional and systemic analyses offered correspond to broader roadmaps for educational reform, such as New Deal and Abolitionist framings that hold more promise for advancing democracy and justice, and thus, this book ends with suggestions for movement building toward such visions.

Advancing justice requires reframing the debate, even and especially among Progressives. Are we ready?

PART I

Historicizing Common Sense

Why schooling, or why are we here in school, or education: Why and for whom and about what and how? These are questions that we should be asking with our students and about our students every day, in and out of school. Although these are questions that have swirled at the heart of struggles throughout the history of schooling, they are also questions that too often lie subdued in public debates about reform, and in the tropes about "why schooling?" that get framed as commonsensical and limit the public imagination.

I was at a conference a few years ago, headlined by a noted journalist who began his keynote casually remarking, as if uncontroversial and incontrovertible, that the primary goal of schooling should be to prepare students to be competitive in the global workforce. He then devoted the bulk of his lecture to describing how schools can do this better than they currently do, for which he received a standing ovation by the hundreds of state, district, and school leaders in the room. I looked around, stunned by the failure of these leaders to challenge the story that schooling is and should be fundamentally in the service of U.S. Capitalism.

By the time of that conference, the United States was already more than a dozen years into No Child Left Behind (NCLB), the 2001 George W. Bush–era reauthorization of the 1965 Elementary and Secondary Education Act (ESEA). NCLB not only changed policy and practice by mandating the standards-and-testing regime that had been emerging since the 1980s, but also changed the narrative about "why schooling?" with a focus on college and career readiness, on preparing children for the future. By treating schools as pipelines for the workforce, it placed value on students, not in and of themselves as children in the now, but rather, as future adults—future workers.

The ideological shift here is significant, as it squarely framed schools as commodities, framed students and teachers as consumers and producers, and framed policies and practices that default to narrow notions of individual responsibility and accountability as not merely most effective, but also most commonsensical. That is, the ideological shift was one that even more squarely positioned the very enterprise of education as being like that of any other industry, to be guided by the Neoliberal tropes that, from the 1970s onward, have implied that there is no alternative.

Neoliberalism? That now-commonsensical notion that the public sector has failed, and that the private sector can do better if education—or healthcare or the economy—were simply to allow and incentivize competition as in a free market.

Such a framing made it more likely that, as federal and state governments disinvest in schools—from reducing allocations by cutting budgets to differently allocating via privatization and vouchers—the public sector would acquiesce and even accept, perhaps because it has come to think of education less and less as a public good and more and more as a commodity that anyone can purchase if they simply work hard enough to afford it. Ironically, supporting such policies that dismantle public education can be done even while repeating the claim that schools are the bedrock of U.S. democracy, that schools provide equal educational opportunity to all, and that schools help to level the playing field and prepare everyone to succeed in life.

This is one of the central paradoxes of schooling: The stated purpose may be to redress inequities, but the function can be to maintain and even widen inequities, and not just as the result of current reforms, but from the very beginning of schooling and by design. The earliest public schools were created for the most elite, and as schools were forced to serve a more diverse population, they created alternative ways to sort, such as through segregation, tracking, disinvestment, labeling, and punishing. *The stated purpose might be equity, democratization, or liberation, but the function has never reached those lofty goals—and was never meant to do so—which is why the so-called achievement gap is not necessarily a sign that schools are failing, but a sign that schools are succeeding at doing exactly what they were set up to do.*

Yet this sorting role of schools is never seamless, uncontested, or entirely effective. Schools and universities are also places where, around the world and throughout history, revolutions have taken seed, because young people are gathered and supported, and the aspiration of justice is in the air, even if the reality contradicts it. Thus, *the purpose-versus-function paradox is not a reason to give up on public education, for just as schools have always served to sort, they also have always served as a central battleground where different sectors struggle to define who we are and what we are to become.*

This is why today's struggles over public education are so vital. Democratizing education demands of us that we dive more deeply into this central paradox, and resist falling victim to the all-too-common tendency of reforms to morph into the newest method of sorting. This task begins with understanding the historical roots of American schooling as an ideological project, which itself requires understanding Americanness as ideological. *To do this, Part I offers several historical renderings—of the construction of Americanness, the roots of mass U.S. schooling, the impact of social movements, the surrenderings of the political Left, and the example of struggles around segregation, school choice, and vouchers—that lay the groundwork for the policy battles of Part II.* We begin with a story of what makes for America.

CONSTRUCTING AMERICANNESS THROUGH OTHERING

American as Western

In 1967, Dr. Martin Luther King, Jr., delivered his "Beyond Vietnam: A Time to Break Silence" speech that would be one of his most controversial, as he spoke out against U.S. participation in the Vietnam War by connecting injustices at home with injustices abroad:

> These are revolutionary times. All over the globe men are revolting against old systems of exploitation and oppression, and out of the wombs of a frail world, new systems of justice and equality are being born. The shirtless and barefoot people of the land are rising up as never before. The people who sat in darkness have seen a great light. We in the West must support these revolutions. It is a sad fact that—because of comfort, complacency, a morbid fear of communism, and our proneness to adjust to injustice—the Western nations that initiated so much of the revolutionary spirit of the modern world have now become the arch anti-revolutionaries. . . . Our only hope today lies in our ability to recapture the revolutionary spirit and go out into a sometimes hostile world declaring eternal hostility to poverty, racism, and militarism. . . . We are now faced with the fact that tomorrow is today. We are confronted with the fierce urgency of now. In this unfolding conundrum of life and history, there is such a thing as being too late.

King's call to revolt against old systems of exploitation and oppression involved connecting the dots between racism at home and racism abroad, between poverty and racism, and between racism and militarism, deepening understanding of the interconnectedness and intersectional nature of injustices. In doing so, his call broadened solidarity with populations across the globe, including the supposed enemy in the Vietnam War that would embody a much longer legacy of servicing Western Imperialism. And that is part of what made his speech so controversial: It linked White supremacy with American Imperialism.

In his 1978 book, *Orientalism*, Edward Said presents a defining theory about Orientalism—an ideology as well as a set of practices that spans two millennia—as an ontological framing of how the West came to understand itself as the West only because and when it defined a whole other part of the world as other-than. Orientalism operates by racializing and sexualizing the Other, characterizing the whole Middle East, the whole of Asia, the whole so-called Orient as racially and sexually very different and deviant through concepts such as its exoticism, mysteriousness, dangerousness, and underdevelopment. Orientalism justified the role of western Europe in colonizing other parts of the world; if others are less than, less developed, less virtuous, then it justifies the more advanced in penetrating, conquering, dominating, and controlling, thus animating a tortured fantasy of a hypermasculinized empire and its feminized, eroticized subject.

In the United States, Orientalism has taken on new life, sometimes called U.S. Orientalism, as manifested in the stereotypes, cultural images, and media representations of Asian American bodies and attributes. These echo the narratives by Western colonizers and profiteers from centuries ago about Asia and Asians as exotic, dangerous, mysterious, unpredictable, and fundamentally different and inferior compared to White western Europeans. *Understanding race and racism, particularly as they concern Asians in the United States—and by implication, Whites in the United States—requires historicizing these stereotypes.*

As Asian immigration increased over time and Asian Americans became a larger population in the United States, new stereotypes would emerge and morph, including the Yellow Peril, the evil and dangerous aliens who prompted fears of Asian invasion and conquest. This stereotype, framed and grounded by Orientalist ideology, emerged historically to serve U.S. Imperialism, justifying exclusion laws in the late 1800s and early 1900s that barred Asian immigration, as well as the incarceration of Japanese Americans during World War II—both events resulting from a mix of racist rhetoric about Asian contamination of communities and families, Asian competition for jobs and market shares, and Asian unassimilability into the United States and underlying loyalty to the enemy.

The racial profiling of Japanese Americans during World War II reverberates today in the context of anti-Muslim rhetoric and discrimination. In the aftermath of the attacks on September 11, 2001, fueled by the scapegoating of Muslims by public officials and the media, fear of and hatred toward Muslims flooded the public discourse. Hate speech, profiling, hate crimes, and other forms of discrimination and harassment increased nationwide, including toward individuals who may not have been Muslim but were perceived to be so. With no acknowledgment of the long histories of U.S.-led violence and harm around the world toward majority-Muslim countries and regions, or of the great diversity within Muslim communities, the dangerousness and un-Americanness of all Muslims was a message unquestioned and promulgated by many. Such messaging continued into 2018 when Trump issued an executive order banning immigration from several majority-Muslim countries, claiming the interest of national security, despite evidence of no such threat.

Several similarities with the incarceration of Japanese Americans are apparent. Against the government's own evidence to the contrary, Japanese Americans were publicly made suspect. Profiling, harassment, threats, violence, and discrimination increased toward anyone suspected of being of Japanese descent, whether or not they were. Widespread incarceration proceeded, with much destruction to property and livelihood. All of these actions materially reinforced the racial Othering of Japanese Americans as fundamentally different, un-American, unable to assimilate or be trusted as American—and therefore inferior, dangerous, and in need of being contained. Indeed, threaded through all such doctored images of Japanese Americans, of Muslims, of the Yellow Peril, and of the Oriental are framings of the Other as different and dangerous, which serve to bolster White supremacy and a racist enclosing and policing of what counts as American.

American as White

In literature, a foil is a character or a storyline that helps to define the protagonist by serving as its contrast or its opposite; that is, the protagonist can be illuminated in opposition to a foil. Language similarly operates through relationship: The concept of *low* is understandable only because there is a contrasting concept of *high*; same with in and out, light and dark, here and there, past and present. Same with identities and groups: Defining some people as good happens only when defining others as bad; there can be a group of *we* only because there are contrasting groups of *them*. Creating an Other—the Othering of others—must constantly happen in order to concretize and stabilize a narrow, exclusive, temporary, contingent sense of self. *National and nationalist identities are no different: Some people count as American only because a whole bunch of Others are made into the non-American, the un-American, the anti-American.*

Not unlike the framing of the West vis-à-vis Orientalism, the framing of Americanness happens only because and only when we construct others as the Other, be they the Yellow Peril, the savage and uncivilized, the unassimilable alien and forever-foreigner, the deviant, the darker, the dangerous. Americanness has always been defined against these constructed Others, using tropes of indigeneity, blackness, brownness, foreignness— all to reinforce, sustain, and police the whitening of Americanness. I remember teaching as a Peace Corps volunteer at a school in a small village in Nepal, where my students asked how I could be American when I was not White; weren't all Americans White, or supposed to be White, at least, the real ones? I remember a TV ad for a Republican White male congressional candidate in Hawai'i decades ago that implied that it was time for our representatives to look "more American"—presumably unlike the Asian Americans, Native Hawaiians, women, and people with disabilities who overwhelmingly and for decades were our senators and representatives in Washington, DC.

To frame Americanness as White is to map whiteness and all that it entails—culturally, politically, linguistically, historically, socially, religiously, biologically, whether based in reality or only presumably so—onto the identity and the body and the livelihood and the collective and the country that is "American." Identifying American as White is to claim these markers and, perhaps more importantly, the privileges and power that come with them, even when—or particularly when—we do not understand how such seemingly beneficial privileges are actually quite dehumanizing to the very ones being privileged.

Therefore, identifying as White is best understood as never ending, iterative, and contested. In being so, the privileges of whiteness are fragile and precarious, at-risk, momentary, and situated, hence the ongoing need to guard, protect, police, and reify such identifications. That is, White privilege, White nationalism, White supremacy—these must be constantly reclaimed and policed, demanding that we constantly Other others, sometimes through violence and force, and other times more subtly and effectively through our stories, like our stories about race as meaningful social categories.

Yet race is not something that just is; rather, it is something that must constantly be remade. Race is something believed by many to be biological in basis, but it is not: Genetically, there is more diversity within race groupings than there is between groups. There is not some biologically based determinant for all that gets attributed to race. What, then, makes for race? A much more helpful and accurate way to think about race is as an instrumental construct, a way to talk about groups in order to advance particular ideologies and systems. People are not already raced; rather, societies racialize for a purpose. This is what makes the Asian-as-foil both volatile and productive—it purports a stable category even as it forces the question, what counts as Asian—and as American—in the here and now?

That race is a social construct becomes more obvious when comparing the different ways that race is defined across different national contexts, such as how *White* is defined differently from country to country, as well as when comparing how race categories changed over time within any given national context. People of Asian descent in the United States are a helpful example: Sometimes they have been grouped as Asian Americans, sometimes they have been grouped as Asian Americans plus Pacific Islanders (AAPIs), and still other times they have been grouped as Asian Americans, Pacific Islanders, plus specifically named subgroups of colonized subjects. This is a naming that makes explicit how, within this very diverse population, there are certain groups that have unique relationships to the United States vis-à-vis colonization and Imperialism, like Native Hawaiians, Filipinx, Guamanians, and Chamorros, and thus they are not quite the same as other AAPIs.

In 1980, the Census changed how it talked about race, and it started using a large, combined category called Asian and Pacific Islander. But 20 years later it decided that, no, these are two very different groups that should be separated into an Asian category and a Native Hawaiian and Other Pacific Islander category. These large groupings, however amalgamated or subdivided, consist of about 22 million people in the United States, encompassing more than 50 countries of heritage with over 100 native languages and with an even larger number of ethnic and cultural groups. It is a vastly diverse group that spans a large geographic portion of the world, each subgroup with unique histories of U.S. relations, including Imperialism, war, resource extraction, labor exploitation, cultural appropriation, and displacement, all impacting both documented and undocumented immigration.

The obscured place of AAPIs in debates about immigration and undocumented immigration further illustrates the instrumental nature of racialization. The Census estimates there to be 22 million AAPIs in this country, about 50% of whom were born outside of this country, which in turn includes about 14% undocumented immigrants. Calculated another way, the Census estimates there to be 11 million undocumented immigrants in this country (some researchers estimate twice as many), 14% of whom identify as AAPI, which is about 1.6 million people. In higher education, the percentages can be much higher: For example, within the University of California system, over 40% of undocumented students are AAPI. Many of the original youth leaders who were organizing for federal legislation to protect undocumented students in the early 2000s were AAPI. Many of the immigrants being targeted, rounded up individually and in groups, and deported are AAPI. Yet, AAPIs are rarely the face of undocumented immigration—why?

Immigrants are a vastly diverse group, consisting of peoples of all races and all regions of the world, and immigration plays a large role in American folklore regarding the founding of this country and the refrain that the United States is a *nation of immigrants*—which is true only by ignoring the Indigenous populations who were colonized and the enslaved populations who were sold and treated as property—who can all partake in the so-called American Dream. *That is, immigration was always a racialized construct: It served particular ideologies by framing in racially specific ways the generic immigrant within any narrative, be that narrative "we are a nation of immigrants" or "we must build a wall to stop illegal immigration."*

Not surprisingly, over time, the posterchild of the immigrant has changed, racializing the body in different ways, all while continually serving White supremacy. Yellow Peril relied on the image of the dangerous Asian immigrant a century ago, just as the image of the Mexican illegally crossing the U.S.–Mexico border today capitalizes on the racist stereotypes, anxieties, and hate directed toward Mexicans; also not unlike the conflation of "the Chinese" with everyone of Asian descent, Mexicans are oftentimes presumed to stand in for all Latin and South Americans. And this shift is purposeful; that is, the erasure of AAPI undocumented immigration helps to magnify Mexicanness as a foil to Americanness at a time when such a contrast is particularly potent.

American as Bordered

The strategic significance of racializing the undocumented as Mexican is perhaps most clear when contextualized in this moment when the American empire is in decline and when the United States is losing its standing as the lone, so-called global superpower. Throughout world history, no empire has dominated the globe for more than a few generations, and as is characteristic of an empire as it struggles to hold on to power, the United States is policing, with increasing investment and demonstrativeness, certain narratives about itself. Even more than exerting military might, controlling the narrative is an incredibly effective way to control a population: Get people to think in only certain ways, and they effectively control themselves. It is why the framing of any story matters—and it is also why any questioning of those stories is dangerous, can upend the very foundations of that empire, and will be vigorously silenced.

In a moment when struggling to gain or retain power, the elite will police with increasing force the sources of possible counterstories, such as the media, science and research, the courts, the arts, and schools and universities, which are the institutions or realms whose primary social function is to inquire and explore, and therefore are precisely the institutions and realms under attack in the United States today.

One such narrative being policed with increasing violence concerns the boundaries between the Us and the Them. Such symbolic differentiation can be made most visceral and stark not at the United States' northern border with another wealthy, predominantly White country, but at the southern border with a poorer, browner country that has long represented a more colonial relationship than one of racial kinship. At that border are staged both material and physical means of differentiation: The building of tall, thick, long walls at that and no other border, and the attacks on anyone who tries to cross that border and trouble the distinction between the Us and the Them, particularly those whose documented or undocumented status is not so easy to see.

By blurring boundaries, the undocumented immigrant bears the brunt of such policing in the forms of caging and abuse, separation of families, surveillance and profiling, criminalization, and deportation. Such attacks had been happening throughout the United States for years, particularly in the years of the Obama administration that ramped up prosecution and deportation. But today, the attacks are most visible and most symbolic at the most visceral of racialized borders, where the current administration frames the crisis as one in which "illegals" brought such inhumane treatment upon themselves.

In the struggle to protect undocumented immigrants, counterstories have not always offered a significant departure from Imperialist ones, even those put forth by Progressives. Examples include the movement to push for passage of a federal Development, Relief, and Education for Alien Minors (DREAM) Act, as well as for family-reunification provisions. The DREAM Act, as drafted but never passed during the Obama administration, would provide for two primary paths toward citizenship—one being college attainment and the other being military service—and proponents have argued that its passage would open and expand the paths toward inclusion and citizenship for more young people.

Undoubtedly, the framing was a pragmatic one that was more likely to get bipartisan support. However, it did so in ways that narrowly defined the good citizen (particularly by privileging military service) and that linked the collective identity of Americans with the increasingly global image of the United States as an expanding empire that used military might to subordinate others. Family-reunification legislation also broadened the available paths toward residency and citizenship, but as with the DREAM Act, it narrowed the definition of the good citizen, in this case, by defining as desirable only those in families that resembled the dominant heteropatriarchal structure.

Rhetoric from the media, politicians, and even activists built on this narrow framing of the good immigrant by narrowly basing the need for immigration reform on deservingness and legality (as in, "they deserve to immigrate here legally"), positioning DREAMers as a new model minority, as a model for all other minorities to aspire toward. Highlighting exemplars of the deserving immigrant, such stories echoed folklore that lay central to the self-identity of the United States as a meritocratic nation, especially the Horatio Alger myth that, if a young man works really hard and persists, he can pull himself out of poverty and achieve the American dream. This is a storyline that got repeated often in education circles as well, including at a fundraiser that I once attended to offer civic engagement and leadership development programs for inner-city youth, where the keynote speaker was an immigrant youth of color who echoed this exact story, effectively tugging at our heartstrings and wallets.

Yes, society should celebrate the accomplishments of youth like this keynote speaker, but significant structural barriers to youth development and academic achievement are masked when success is credited entirely to the efforts of the individual. Such a framing demands conformity: By saying that only those immigrants who play by the rules are deserving, advocates indirectly close off the possibility that immigrants who, say, protest and challenge those rules, also fit and should fit into the fabric of U.S. democracy. Protest and political activism are as much a part of the identity and the values of the United States as is fitting in and obeying.

This is also true with the narrative that good immigrants contribute to the economy—they pay taxes, they spend as consumers—and are needed for economic productivity and growth, as they often take on the jobs that other groups do not want to do. Such a framing of the contributing individual detracts from the much larger, systemic problems: A value system that demeans entire categories of work and, in turn, entire categories of workers and consumers; a U.S.-driven globalized economy that is of enormous benefit to only a very small percent of the people in this world; U.S.-led initiatives—economic sanctions, military and political interventions—that devastated economies, increased political instability, and displaced people around the world—all problems that are actually furthered by U.S. immigration policy.

Americanness is a project inseparable from Imperialism, White supremacy, and Nationalism. It entitles some, as it Others others. It does so through any number of its institutions, be they legal, medical, religious, economic, social, educational. And it does so by design, and from its very beginnings, making any of these projects—particularly schooling—quintessentially "American."

ROOTS AND FORCES SHAPING EARLY U.S. SCHOOLING

From the late 1700s to the early 1900s, countries throughout western Europe developed mass schooling systems, which is sometimes described as one of the defining features of modernization; a society becomes more advanced when its people become more educated. Mass schooling systems fulfilled a political purpose in nation building, both internally and externally: Externally, a number of European countries continued to expand their empires and colonize others around the world, particularly in the global south; internally, many European countries underwent the First Industrial Revolution, from agrarian to industrial economies, around the start of the 19th century and the Second Industrial Revolution, from human labor to fueled machinery, around the start of the 20th century. During the second revolution, the building of infrastructure for mass transportation as well as of massive complexes of factories and workplaces drew migrations internally and immigration from abroad into what would become large urban cities.

Whether colonizing or urbanizing abroad or within, a similar problem arose: how to control a rapidly growing, far more diverse population than the wealthier, White, ruling elite. Hence the development of mass schooling and the exporting of such schooling forms with the purpose to socialize, as illustrated by the differentiated structure and curriculum of schools for the elite versus for the masses or the colonized, as well as the pervasiveness of Christian teachings within the formal curriculum as the basis for moral instruction. Schools were arms of the state for the express purpose of socialization, teaching students to fit into only particular, supposedly appropriate places within the economic, social, and other hierarchies that permeated their societies. Schools were colonizing minds, and in so doing, were teaching students to control themselves.

Common Schools

Modeled after the systems of western Europe, the United States too developed mass schooling systems, albeit a little more slowly. Until the late 1700s in the colonies that would become the United States, academic teaching and learning, particularly of literacy and numeracy, happened only rarely by hired tutors in wealthier families or in churches for those in religious study, which meant that for most children, it was not happening at all. In the last decades of the 1700s, soon after the birth of the United States, New England saw the emergence of what would become a thriving movement of *common schools,* which were the predecessors to public schools.

Typified by the one-room schoolhouse—with, say, one or two dozen boys of mixed ages under the supervision of one teacher—common schools were public in some ways, as they were open and free to certain boys throughout a particular community, and private in some ways, often being privately funded and run, at least in part. Not surprisingly, they were quite elitist: Created by wealthy Whites, the schools served their own, meaning they primarily served children who were male, who were White, and whose families owned property. This exclusiveness of the common schools persisted for the next century, but there were exceptions: Over time more girls were "smuggled" in, and although common schools never came to integrate Black students, a handful of separate schools opened for Black children who were not enslaved.

By the mid-1800s, common schools had spread across the country, a movement often credited to the vision and leadership of Horace Mann, an educator, lawyer, and elected leader from Massachusetts, known for calling education "the great equalizer of the conditions of men," who pushed for open, free schools with a common curriculum and structure. One thread across common schools was the curricular focus on moral instruction. The most common textbook for decades was the *McGuffey Reader,* which taught students to read by using fire-and-brimstone stories about how people will perish in hell if they did not follow the teachings of the Christian church, particularly a native Protestantism. Moral education and socialization figured centrally from early on, intertwined with and inseparable from academics, and this was the foundation on which public schooling would build.

Mass Schooling Systems

The end of the Civil War and Reconstruction coincided with the beginning of the Second Industrial Revolution in the United States, and it was in this period that mass public school systems emerged. That is, in the last few decades of the 1800s through the early 1900s, public school systems (publicly funded and run) developed across the country, fueled by the Second Industrial Revolution and its concomitant growth of large cities, of infrastructure for transportation, of immigration from Europe, and soon, of the Great Migration of African Americans out of the South. Given the emergence of a much more diverse and poorer population, it is not surprising that the schools that developed in urban centers looked nothing like the schools that were developed a century earlier for the elite.

Modeled more after factories than after homes in both governance and organization, the schools were highly compartmentalized—dividing students by age, by gender, and by ability; dividing curriculum by subject and time, into the Carnegie units, which ultimately remains how schools compartmentalize curriculum today; dividing communities by race via segregated schools; and differentiating what students learned and experienced based on these divisions. For example, the curricular differentiation by gender was—well, highly gendered, particularly by tailoring subject areas, technical skills, and extracurricular activities to prepare girls for domestic work and boys for the paid workforce. Similar curricular differentiation existed by age, ability, and race as well.

The rapid expansion of public school systems across the country coincided with the Jim Crow era and legal segregation, so this period was also defined by the growth of an apartheid school system, in which the problem, as recognized by the Supreme Court in its 1954 *Brown v. Board of Education* decision, was not merely that students were separated, but also that the schools for Black students were unquestionably and systemically inferior and, as such, discriminatory.

This designed inferiority was manifest not only in resource allocation, but also in curriculum content. In 1933, well before *Brown*, Carter G. Woodson's *The Mis-Education of the Negro* argued that schools were teaching Black students not just less content, but content that was ideologically problematic: Schools were teaching students to view the world through a White lens, thereby teaching Black students to fit into an inferior position within the racial hierarchy of the United States. For Woodson, the solution should not be to teach students even more of this problematic curriculum, but rather, to teach students a fundamentally different curriculum.

This colonizing role of schooling is visible in the schools and curriculum created for other racialized groups as well, including schools in Hawai'i in the late 1800s and early 1900s that aimed to teach native Hawaiian and Asian immigrant children to both denationalize and to Americanize—that is, to disidentify with Hawai'i and Asian countries of origin while embracing dominant American worldviews and values. The same is true of the boarding schools for Indigenous students, which were modeled after the military and led, in part, by military leaders, that proliferated throughout the country in the late 1800s and early 1900s, which aimed to "kill the Indian, save the man" by teaching students to lose the parts that society devalues—Indigenous culture, language, family ties, identity—in order to fit into American society, albeit at an inferior, subordinate, underserved place within.

Socialization does not aim for the same outcome for all students; rather, it teaches some that they belong at the top and others that they belong at the bottom, and teaches all that this order is the way that society should be. In so doing, schools sort. They sort via excluding some students from schools in the first place, via segregating schools, via tracking classrooms, but perhaps most insidiously—and yet most enduringly throughout history—via what they teach and to whom, the stories they tell, and the subtle ways that they silence any counterstories.

Evolution of the Teaching Profession

Even the images of who should be teaching our children reflected the sorting, assimilating purpose of schools. There were contexts in which schools wanted men to teach, especially to the older students, because men, presumably, would make for smarter, stricter teachers than women. There were contexts in which schools wanted women to teach, especially to the younger students, because as long as the primary grades were modeled after the home, the teachers could be more motherly, more in loco parentis. There were contexts in which schools wanted, for several reasons, only younger women to teach: Women were expected eventually to get married and fulfill their social obligation of being a wife and mother, so too many women in the teaching force would destabilize the home and the workplace; additional fears abounded of strong older women emasculating boys or serving as a model of deviant sexuality—spinster, lesbian—for girls, which is a fear of sexual contamination by teachers that has reverberated to the present.

Intersected with gender and sexuality was race, for the idealized image of the teacher was not just any women, but a woman who was White. This image has persisted in the overall demographics of the teaching profession for the past century, thus suggesting that the concerted efforts to diversify over the past few decades may be failing because this ideological underpinning remains intact.

However, just as schools have always been sites of contestation, so has the role of teachers. The teaching profession, in some ways servicing the sorting function of schools, has also been arguably the most significant force to improve and democratize school systems, particularly through their long history of unions and teacher-led advocacy.

The National Education Association (NEA) formed in 1857 (as the National Teachers Association), initially as a professional association that focused on legislative and policy advocacy, but in the early-to-mid 1900s it would gradually evolve into a union of teachers and other school personnel, engaging more forcefully in collective bargaining and pushed to the Left in order to compete with the American Federation of Teachers (AFT). The AFT formed in 1916, primarily by teachers in Chicago who were frustrated with the priorities of the NEA. From its origins, the AFT focused on improving the conditions for teachers, and through their advocacy and bargaining, demonstrated the impact of teachers acting collectively, and teachers' widespread desire to do so. In subsequent decades, the AFT would align with the more inclusive, Socialist, and militant industrial-union organizing of the Congress of Industrial Organizations (CIO), pushing the profession to the Left in the same way the CIO pushed labor organizing in general to the Left.

The growth of the labor movement in the late 1950s, in concert with the thrust of the Civil Rights Movement, provided fertile ground for the heyday of teacher unions. The NEA and the AFT supported teachers in over 1,000 strikes in the 1960s and early 1970s, demanding, among other things, better pay and conditions for teachers. Teacher unions would emerge as one of the leading public-sector unions seeing growth in membership and activity and, together, the NEA and AFT would account for over 70% of public school teachers being protected by collective bargaining agreements. Although initially divided or outright resistant, the two unions would eventually support school desegregation, as well as increased and targeted federal funding to address education inequities and disparities, and other core initiatives of the Civil Rights Movement and the War on Poverty. They worked to integrate their own ranks, as when the White-dominated NEA merged with the American Teachers Association, a union serving Black schools in the South, in

1966. Together, the memberships of NEA and AFT would grow into the millions.

However, from the 1980s onward, strikes became increasingly rare. The historically more militant AFT would gradually lose such a reputation, instead establishing patterns of trying to work within various reforms, as its counterpart the NEA came to be seen as a bit more of an outspoken critic of reforms. This contrast was exemplified in the different strategies that each took following the passage of No Child Left Behind in 2001. But regardless of whether and how each union voiced public opinions, the collective and public action of both declined steadily, that is, until 2012.

Almost 100 years after the founding of the AFT and its Leftward push in teacher organizing, it would again be teachers in Chicago—this time, the AFT affiliate, Chicago Teachers Union (CTU), in its 2012 and 2019 strikes—who would lead another major shift in union priorities and strategy. *The CTU insisted on engaging in collective bargaining "for the common good," which would highlight the broader conditions needed for quality schools, not merely teacher compensation, as well as a return to the grassroots organizing, public consciousness raising, and collective action and striking that defined the strategies of unions from earlier in the twentieth century. Such a strategy departed from the acquiescence to austerity demands that predominated union tendencies in the decades since the Conservative movement of the 1980s, when many felt such compromises to be the most pragmatic as public sector unions faced increasing attacks and saw their legal protections weakened.*

The 1980s, however, was not the first time that the attack on unions forced a retreat. That precedent was set in the 1950s, in the early years of the Cold War, when Communist-baiting pushed unions and the broader Left to surrender—a story that would happen several times in the decades since, and thus, a story worth exploring in more detail.

A Turning Point

Accompanying the long history of schooling as an instrument to socialize and sort is an equally long and vibrant history of both large and small struggles to define what should be taught in schools, and how, and to whom, and by whom, and for what purpose. But up to the mid-1900s, public schools were still primarily a state and local endeavor with little oversight at the federal level and with relatively little nationwide organizing beyond teacher unions. It would be following pivotal global and national events of the 1940s and 1950s that the struggles over public education became intertwined with—or a centerpiece of—several competing social movements.

The Cold War and the Space Race were bubbling since the end of World War II, but Russia's launch of the first outer space satellite, *Sputnik I*, in 1957 gave its U.S. rival a crisis in identity and in confidence, and attention at the U.S. federal level turned to the educational system, questioning whether it was falling short of serving our Imperialist ambitions, with calls for more investment in science and technology. Such a crisis also led to the expansion of the military–industrial complex—armed forces, technology, auxiliary services, and other industries that are needed for conventional war—as well as expansion of apparatuses for engaging in hybrid wars, which are any combination of military, political, economic, cultural, and other interventions with the same goal to dominate. One of the most common and effective hybrid-war apparatuses to be waged in the decades since was and is economic warfare, as through sanctions, embargoes, tariffs, and contingent loans, which were actions that not only aligned with, but also were propelled by, the U.S. corporate sector's eye toward global hegemony.

Thus, the 1950s was also a time of the growing influence of free-market economics and Neoliberal ideology, espoused and promulgated most notably by economist Milton Friedman and his students and colleagues in the economics department at the University of Chicago. Neoliberalism was an ideology that would quickly come to dominate U.S. foreign policy and policies of the major international economic bodies, as well as the internal U.S. economy and related sectors, as detailed, for example, in the writings by Friedman in 1955 on the role of the federal government in public education that helped lay the theoretical and rhetorical groundwork for school vouchers.

But it was shortly before that, and not unrelated, that the 1954 *Brown* decision would signal the beginning of a string of federal actions—and would constitute an even larger string of civil rights activism and Conservative backlash and Neoliberal framing—that would mark schools as preeminent sites of ideological struggle and related reforms. The groundwork for *Brown* began years earlier with such precedent-setting cases in lower courts as *Mendez v. Westminster*, in which the Ninth Circuit Court of Appeals ruled in 1947 that segregated schooling for Mexican Americans in California violated the 14th Amendment. Even before that, nationwide organizing and movement building had been happening for decades by organizations playing a sizable role in seeding or leading what would become the Civil Rights Movement.

It is not coincidental that the high-profile court cases on desegregation would happen from the mid-1940s to the mid-1950s. These cases exemplify the framing of civil rights activism that had much to do with the

Cold War and, in particular, the Second Red Scare and McCarthyism—public accusations, demonization, and criminalization of anyone deemed on the Left, which was conflated with Communism—of the late 1940s and the 1950s.

The Civil Rights Movement originally had a broader goal. Post–World War II, the leading civil rights organizations strategized ways to present a case to the new United Nations Commission on Human Rights that charged the United States with violating the human rights of its Black citizens, as evidenced by the pervasiveness of poverty, their disenfranchisement from government, and the inferiority of their healthcare and educational provisions. But the emergence of the Cold War suppressed and silenced criticisms of the U.S. government by labeling such criticisms un-American and Communist ploys to subvert democracy. *It was this fear of being dismissed and persecuted as Communist that prompted, at least in part, a retreat from broader human rights to a narrower civil rights agenda that focused on the right to be free from discrimination and treated equally in public sectors.* This strategy would lead to many legislative and legal victories and a fundamental change in the role of the federal government in education, but it was a compromised strategy, and thus, a compromised stance for what would reveal itself to be a fragile Left.

World War II ended in 1945, and President Franklin D. Roosevelt died in office that same year. The Liberal socio-economic policies embodied in the New Deal of the Roosevelt administration had long angered the Conservative wing of the Democratic Party. As the 1944 election approached, Roosevelt's rapidly declining health spurred Conservatives to act in order to ensure that the even more Liberal vice president, Henry Wallace, whose positions seemed too Communist to some, was not still vice president if Roosevelt were to die in office in his fourth term. Despite the popularity of the incumbent Wallace among both the public and the delegates, Conservatives mounted a campaign that successfully turned Roosevelt against Wallace, and then maneuvered the convention to secure the votes of the delegates to put the far more moderate Harry Truman on the ballot. As expected, Roosevelt was elected to a fourth term, and then died the following year. The New Deal priorities would end, and the Democratic Party would remain squarely centrist for decades to come.

The Civil Rights Movement and the Federal Era

Prior to *Brown*, the federal government played a minimal role in public education, leaving it to state and local officials to oversee schools, and in so doing, allowing apartheid schooling to persist. What finally forced the federal government to begin to enforce constitutional protections against discrimination by race was the massive uprising of the Civil Rights Movement, accompanied by legal strategists and litigators who set precedent in lower courts spanning more than a decade prior, culminating in one of the first major legal victories of the movement: The *Brown v. Board of Education* case, a consolidation of four separate cases in which the U.S. Supreme Court ruled that segregated schools were inherently unequal and that a segregated system violated the Equal Protection Clause of the 14th Amendment of the U.S. Constitution. A year later, in 1955, the Court issued its *Brown II* ruling that states must proceed "at all deliberate speed" to desegregate, which was a weak and unfunded mandate that called on states to desegregate, but with no deadline, guidelines, support, or consequences, and not surprisingly, with little impact and little change resulting in schools over the next decade.

Civil rights advocacy continued, with increased attention on legislation that would compel action and change, particularly the leveraging of federal funding—that is, the threat to withhold federal funds—in order to compel compliance with nondiscrimination law. This was the precedent set by the Civil Rights Act of 1964, soon to be followed by the ESEA of 1965, which are the legislations credited with propelling forward desegregation, particularly for Black students in the South for the next quarter century. Following ESEA was a string of major laws that addressed other, intersected forms of discrimination in public schools, including the Bilingual Education Act of 1968, the Education Amendments of 1972 that included Title IX on sex discrimination, and the Education for All Handicapped Children Act of 1975 (later called the Individuals with Disabilities Education Act, or IDEA).

Litigation continued throughout this period as well, leading to such landmark cases as the *Lau v. Nichols* case of 1974, in which the U.S. Supreme Court distinguished between equal treatment—in this case, teaching in English to all students—and equitable outcomes, whereby all students can understand and learn, regardless of language background. By recognizing that different students have different capacities and needs, the Court mandated that school districts accommodate English language learners lest they fail to provide equal educational opportunity, thus making explicit that discrimination can happen when schools fail to provide additional support to those who need it.

It is this period, from the mid-1950s through the 1970s, that is called the Federal Era in U.S. education because of the significant intervention by and influence of the federal government through legislation and the courts, culminating in the 1979 creation of the U.S. Department of

Education, which resulted from bringing together several smaller offices that were spread across various departments, elevating this new department to cabinet level, and quickly expanding it. *The role of the federal government was both expansive and narrow: Expansive in its focus on elaborating a vision and holding states accountable for advancing that vision of public schools as embodiments of democracy, civil rights, and equity; but narrow in its focus on antidiscrimination law, and not, for example, on reparations or curriculum.*

The Civil Rights Movement did not limit itself in the same way: Its gains were varied and significant, reaching far beyond its legislative and legal victories, which is not surprising, given that social movements are defined by their ability to change not merely policy and law, but also public consciousness and common sense. Leaders, strategists, organizers, and activists within the movement recognized that a society can change only when—or especially when—the dominant stories that have long colonized our minds become troubled, and when critical, skeptical, imaginative inquiries prompt us to seek counterstories and resist the assimilative demand to conform and self-control. For this reason, they also attended deeply to curriculum.

Curriculum is not merely that which the elite predetermine to be the knowledge and skills most important to pass down. *More broadly, curriculum can and should be that which is not yet known, or rattles what is already known, or asks what is it that society might come to know and be, making the process of defining curriculum one that is never divorced from larger struggles over identity, knowledge, values, and ideology.*

Examples of curricular initiatives outside of the public schools included the Citizenship Schools, which by the early 1960s had burgeoned across the South to teach literacy and citizenship rights to African Americans in order to foster civic engagement and democratic participation, spearheaded by Septima Clark, who oversaw the establishment of about 1,000 schools and trained about 10,000 leaders. Similar were the Freedom Schools, launched in the Freedom Summer of 1964 by the Student Nonviolent Coordinating Committee (SNCC) to counter the "sharecropper," conformist education of mainstream schooling by raising critical consciousness about issues of inequities in society. The Freedom School movement started with several dozens of schools in that first summer, and then multiplied as they inspired other such alternative political education spaces in the years and decades to come, with Freedom Schools in operation even today, modeled after those from half a century ago.

Both the Citizenship Schools and the Freedom Schools drew directly on the strategies and resources of the Highlander Folk School, a center in Appalachia that trained leaders and organizers of social movements, beginning with the CIO and the organized labor movement of the 1930s and 1940s, and continuing with the Civil Rights Movement of the 1950s and 1960s. Not surprisingly, both the Citizenship and Freedom Schools offered an education that blended academic instruction with political education; was open to youth and adults; convened in any number of public and private spaces, such as church basements, private lawns and garages, backrooms of businesses, and community spaces; were typically of no cost to students and no pay for teachers; and were interconnected with the vast networks of similar schools in order to share curriculum, resources, and outreach strategies.

The Civil Rights Movement also impacted public school curriculum, as with the call for multicultural education and the critique of traditional curriculum that centered and elevated whiteness, misrepresented people of color and other marginalized groups, and obscured the role of structural injustices in U.S. society, especially in and through the study of history, literature, and other forms of cultural production. Communities were calling for curriculum to be reflective of the diversity of our country, relevant to students' lives and the problems and injustices that their communities face, and tailored to elements such as their ways of knowing, interests, and abilities.

Not surprisingly, achievement by race was changing: When looking at standardized test scores, the so-called achievement gap—that is, the gap between, on one level, the aggregate test scores of White and Asian American students, and, on a much lower level, the aggregate for Black, Latinx, Indigenous, and Pacific Islander students—and especially the White–Black gap, was closing in the 2 decades from the mid-1960s to the early 1980s.

Higher education curriculum was also changing as a result of organizing, as with the Third World Liberation Front strikes and the push to decolonize, decenter whiteness, and expand ethnic studies. Ethnic studies is sometimes narrowly described as curriculum about people of color, about the margins, but its origins reveal a much broader scope of analysis to include the center—that is, not merely the honoring of diversity, but also the critical analysis of normalcy and the normative demand to conform and acquiesce. Today, battles over curriculum in public schools echo loudly these early interventions of ethnic studies in higher education, as exemplified by the recent and ongoing struggle in Tucson, Arizona, over the banning of the Mexican American Studies program, with critics claiming that ethnic studies' critique of White hegemony is akin to teaching students to be anti-American, or that its honoring of diversity is akin to teaching separatism and exclusion.

BIPARTISAN CONVERGENCE

Clearly, as major transformations unfolded in policy, curriculum, and consciousness, some were not having it. Laying the groundwork for this retreat from the gains of the Civil Rights Movement were other social movements whose ideologies of American exceptionalism, Capitalist democracy, Conservatism, militarism, and Neoliberalism would so compellingly frame education as to make indistinguishable the Republican agenda from the Democratic one. Several key events of the 1970s created just the right mindset for this bipartisan convergence.

Trepidation by Liberals

The Civil Rights Movement pushed not only Conservatives but also Moderates and Liberals to question fundamental assumptions about what makes for a democratic society, perhaps most starkly in the ways that the Democratic administrations in the 1960s of Presidents Kennedy and Johnson were constantly facing pressure to do more to address systemic, structural racism and injustice. These administrations self-identified and were identified by others as more Liberal, more in solidarity with people of color than Republicans and even the mainstream of America. The challenge to the status quo by a large social movement was not singular to the United States at this time, for the 1960s was a time of mass uprisings and social unrest in nearly every continent of the world, including in both Imperialist and third-world countries as well as by Indigenous nations. Throughout history, there have been struggles and unrest in and from the margins, but the 1960s struggles were unusually salient because they occurred at a time when democratic, Capitalist nations wanted to frame their economic and governmental structures as more favorable to the masses than Communist ones.

It was thus in 1974 that the Trilateral Commission, a product of the Cold War that brought together three democratized regions—Japan, western European countries, and the United States (whose team included individuals who would go on to serve in the Democratic administration of President Carter later that decade)—issued a report that argued that this global phenomenon of civil unrest was the result of "too much democracy," too much of a sense among the masses that they should have the same as the elite, and further, that such discontent was the result of mass schooling's failure to serve its central purpose of socialization.

From this perspective, the curricular transformations of the Civil Rights Movement exemplified how consciousness raising threatens the social order, which, yes, was precisely the goal by the movement, but was also why some Liberal Democrats wanted to retreat, particularly in the midst of the Cold War. Although this stance of Liberals to decry the failings of public education was shaped at the time by that political context, it would nonetheless reverberate for decades to come, making their stance peculiarly open to aligning with the burgeoning Conservative reframing of education.

Backlash by Conservatives

The Civil Rights Movement demonstrated how long-term planning, collective action, strategic framing, and mass mobilizing can indeed transform both public consciousness and policy. Some critics wondered what it would mean for a countermovement not merely to retreat from the gains of the Civil Rights Movement, but, more proactively, to build toward a very different vision of what U.S. society could look like. In particular, what could society look like by flipping the script on who should rule, such that the goal would no longer be to empower the masses, but to strengthen the civic impact of the corporate elite?

Toward this end, the Conservative revolution that would come to take over the White House in 1980 with the election of Ronald Reagan actually began more quietly a decade earlier, in the early 1970s, with various groups coalescing for a common purpose and against a common enemy. The purpose was to challenge the legal and cultural changes regarding race, social class, gender, and other social markers that were brought about by the Civil Right Movement, the War on Poverty, the feminist movement, and other movements in the 1950s and 1960s; and the enemy, at least early on, was the "Liberal establishment" that steered and supported these movements. What galvanized and guided the early organizing was the 1971 Powell Manifesto, a memo internal to the U.S. Chamber of Commerce written by Lewis Powell, who soon after became an Associate Justice on the U.S. Supreme Court. The memo articulated this common enemy and purpose in its description of a concerted Liberal attack on the so-called American free enterprise system, the U.S. political economy, and on American democracy itself, and the resulting need to organize.

In response to the Powell Manifesto, a group of Conservatives, particularly philanthropists with family-business fortunes, formed in 1971 the Philanthropy Roundtable that would strategize how to use their wealth for Conservative movement building. In the decades to follow, they would develop interconnected funding priorities or strategies to advance public policy agendas that were pro-business and anti-social welfare, seeding what would become an expansive network of think tanks, advocacy organizations, lobbyists, media institutions, and educational entities that worked synergistically to change law and common sense. A year later, in 1972, the Republican Study Committee would form as the heart of Conservative strategizing within Congress.

The year 1972 also saw the formation of the Business Roundtable that would bring together 300 of the top CEOs in the United States with the goal of shaping economic and social policy to support profits for individual corporations, as well as global dominance by the broader U.S. sector. Public education is the primary pipeline of workers, and unsurprisingly, the Business Roundtable soon targeted educational policy. In 1989, it released a report, *Essential Components of a Successful Educational System*, offering "essential principles" that would shape how to think of educational improvement in terms of narrow, rigid articulations of standards and accountability, bolstering and guiding the high-stakes testing regime that was already shaping educational reform. The Business Roundtable helped to frame the crisis of public schools in terms of student achievement, launching a national obsession with "closing the achievement gap" that would shape the agendas of even Left-leaning organizations like the teachers unions for the next quarter century and, in so doing, mask systemic and structural injustices by framing the problem and solution in terms of individual performance and accountability.

By the 1980s, the expansion and transformation of traditional curriculum via multicultural education and ethnic studies that happened in the 1960s and 1970s would be countered by the call for a national curriculum, the "back to basics" movement, the standards-and-testing movement, and the focus on "closing the achievement gap." Such initiatives demanded a retreat from multicultural education, a narrowing and standardizing of curriculum, and a return to the framings of what students should learn and how they should be taught that animated the national imaginary of a golden era now lost, a time when things used to be better, not derailed and thwarted by desegregation and civil rights—and, for that matter, by women's liberation, queer liberation, antiwar organizing, and the War on Poverty.

Not surprisingly, this curricular retreat happened in the same decade when the retreat from *Brown* was in full effect—that is, when many of the court orders that mandated desegregation programs across the country were being allowed or even pushed to expire. By the end of the 1980s, public schools entered a period of resegregation, returning to the use of residence as the basis for school assignment and, as a result, given the trend for neighborhoods to increasingly segregate, schools have become not merely as segregated as they were pre-*Brown*, but in some places, even more so today.

The 1980s was also immediately after the formation of the new federal Department of Education in 1979, which had been opposed by Republicans, but would offer a platform and resources to push forward Conservative framings and initiatives. The Reagan Administration's 1983 report, *A Nation at Risk*, fueled the rhetoric of national insecurity in the midst of the Cold War, a weakening economy in the midst of global competition, and growing inequity and unrest. Such concerns were attributed to an educational system that was failing and pointed to the need to raising standards; holding schools and educators more accountable, and through testing; attaching higher stakes to test scores; centralizing decisionmaking, while disenfranchising communities; standardizing curriculum, while deprofessionalizing teachers; and, of course, restructuring school systems and accountability systems to be modeled after more effective industries and sectors—in particular, the free-market economy.

This Conservative framing of the problem and solution would so compellingly frame the debate on public schooling that both Republicans and Democrats would push forward policies and initiatives in the decades to come that took the United States even more deeply toward such a vision with each new iteration, from Clinton's Goals 2000 to Bush's No Child Left Behind—which was sponsored by one of the most Liberal Democrats in Congress, Senator Ted Kennedy, and parts of which were drafted in the final years of the Clinton administration by Democratic appointees and staff—to Obama's Race to the Top. Importantly, the effectiveness of this Conservative framing resulted not merely from the retreat from civil rights, but also from the parallel move toward a particular way of thinking about system improvement and fairness, as embodied in Neoliberalism and free-market economics.

By the 1980s, both Republicans and Democrats were supporting policy initiatives that placed great faith on the market and competition to drive system improvement, whether that system was the economy or education. This so-called Washington Consensus privileged, at least rhetorically, certain structures or conditions as necessary for success—such as fiscal austerity, privatization, market liberalization, individual accountability that incentivized entrepreneurialism, and system deregulation and decentralization that disincentivized market controls—while obscuring the contradictions that coexisted. Such contradictions include grossly subsidizing some as others face austerity, or the over-regulation of some as others enjoy under- or deregulation, or punishing some while others on the same team and bearing more responsibility get bailed out, all of which exemplify how the commonsensical frames of best or necessary practices insidiously obscure the intentionally disparate impact that these reforms were designed to have on the elite versus the masses.

Another Retreat of the Left

This bipartisan convergence was cemented in 1991 with the widely trumpeted triumph of Capitalist democracy over Communism. The 1989 fall of the Berlin Wall, the 1989 occupation and massacre in Tiananmen Square, and especially the 1991 collapse of the Soviet Union displayed for all the world to see the giants of the Communist Bloc in disarray, just as the two Capitalist powers were reaching the height of their Conservative revolutions—that is, as the United States and United Kingdom neared a decade of the Reagan–Thatcher era. The end of the Cold War sparked several profound global changes.

The collapse of the Soviet Union would remove Communism as the central foil for Capitalism, thus creating a vacuum ideologically in place of the image against which Capitalist democracies had defined themselves post–World War II. Seeing itself as an uncontested global superpower, the United States would soon create a new foil, a vague enemy of U.S. Capitalism, broadly defined as anyone who threatened American democracy and self-interest, a global terror that would justify the unprecedented expansion of the military–industrial complex for a war that demanded ongoing Imperialist intervention worldwide against an enemy that was neither definable nor containable—that is, a war that would, by definition, be global and without end.

This Neoconservative equating of global security with the interests of the corporate elite broadened the scope of U.S. democracy to include Imperialist expansion without regard to other nations' boundaries or relationships to the United States—thus justifying our intervention anywhere, even within the borders of our allies—at the same time that it severely narrowed the identity of U.S. democracy by framing any critique of the U.S. economy as antipatriotic and a sign of loyalty to the Communism already defeated. *In an era when the mainstream Left—the Democratic Party, labor unions, civil rights organizations—was already becoming more centrist, the fall of Communism prompted much of the Far Left to surrender or go underground, such as Communists, Socialist Democrats, Anarchists, and others who historically figured centrally in leading, organizing, envisioning, and otherwise building the Leftist social movements of the 20th century.*

Parallel to the 1940s, Communist-baiting and new forms of blacklisting once again put the Left in retreat. It is difficult to imagine what labor organizing and union building would have looked like in the early and mid-1900s without Communists doing as much of the organizing as they did, or without Marxism shaping much of the analysis and strategy, just as with the Civil Rights Movement, Black radicalism, the feminist movement, the queer movement, the War on Poverty, and the antiwar movement. But post-1991, as the Republican Party became more Conservative, so too did the Democratic Party, and not surprisingly, those Democrats who have since led from the White House would be notably more centrist and Neoliberal than any other Democratic administration since the dawn of Neoliberalism.

Reign of Neoliberalism

That Conservatives and Liberals clash on policy specifics even as both default to Neoliberal assumptions reveals just how commonsensical and pervasive Neoliberalism has become, making it vitally important to understand its origins.

Post–World War II, as the United States gained dominance in the global financial institutions (World Bank, International Monetary Fund), and as its own treasury itself became a major global player, the United States thrusted free-market economics into international policy, particularly by leveraging funds to push for Neoliberal reforms worldwide. Beginning in the 1940s, but mainly in the 1950s and 1960s, time and again, as countries fell into economic turmoil and sought help, the global financial institutions withheld support unless these countries agreed to implementing fiscal austerity, deregulation, and the other conditions that would transform their economies to look more and more like a free market. Rhetorically, such reforms would improve the economy, but for whom?

Such conditions were never about democratizing systems or redistributing income and resources with an eye toward equity—and in fact, such conditions were precisely in opposition to these goals that sounded too Socialist. No, such conditions were designed to increase and differentiate opportunities to profit, which by definition meant that some would get even wealthier as others would get even poorer. The Conservative Reaganomics concept in the 1980s of trickle down economics, in which subsidizing the top would somehow lead to wealth trickling down to the masses, was apropos even here. And, like in the 1980s in the United States, as well as with the multitrillion dollar Obama-era bank bailout in 2009, or the Trump-era tax cuts at an unprecedented level for the wealthiest in 2017, such rhetoric was completely disconnected from the reality. Time after time, the free-market reforms led to greater wealth gaps and disparities—that is, to even greater numbers in poverty and greater amounts of concentrated wealth for the elite than before.

This imperative to marketize was applied not only to economic policy, but to other sectors as well, including educational reform, particularly in Latin American countries in the 1970s when the global financial institutions began to make financial loans contingent on the deregulation and privatization of public schools, purporting that such marketizing and competition will drive effort, innovation, and improvement. But predictably, what began as some of the highest literacy rates in the world would quickly nosedive at the same time that achievement gaps and educational inequities expanded, exactly in line with the expansion of wealth gaps in those countries. This should not be surprising; in a competition, there cannot help but be winners and losers, and while the rhetoric might promise that wealth will trickle down, the reality is that the subsidizing of the top only enables the top to continue winning.

As if all of this was not bad enough, what often followed was the U.S. corporate sector profiteering off of the devastation that it helped to bring about in other countries through what journalist and author Naomi Klein has called "disaster capitalism" in her 2007 book, *Shock Doctrine. The cycle of exacerbating inequity through marketization and then profiteering off of the resulting disaster—which then leads to even more inequity and even more profiteering—increases both the dominance of one side and the subservience of the other, and thus, is fundamentally an Imperialist project, and is so by design.*

Similarly, within the United States, Neoliberalism was shaping not only economic policy, but educational policy as well, and this strategic cycle of crisis–marketize–profiteer would emerge as one of the most effective and enduring frames to reinscribe dominance–subservience and to counter the gains of the Civil Rights Movement, starting with one of its earliest and most significant gains: desegregation.

The Case of School Choice and Vouchers

Post-*Brown*, it would not take long for opponents of desegregation to find a policy proposal that would make mandatory desegregation programs sound unnecessary by offering a seemingly more organic alternative: school choice. Students and their parents of all racial backgrounds will want to get into the best schools, making the marketization of and competition for schools a more natural means of desegregating, or so the rhetoric went. In reality, school choice programs do not desegregate schools, but quite the opposite—they have proven to exacerbate racial segregation—which is not surprising because the rhetoric of school choice as a means to desegregate belies the reality that it was never designed to desegregate, and instead, was proffered precisely to avoid desegregating.

The commonsensical-sounding rhetoric that marketization can offer a solution to racial injustice shows just how seductive Neoliberalism can be as it masks the White supremacy that underlies the intent. After all, school choice was not only about keeping racialized groups separate; it was also about keeping wealthy Whites at the top, and sustaining or even expanding their political, social, and economic advantage. The battle to desegregate, as with so much of the Civil Rights Movement, was about toppling White supremacy, not just getting along with neighbors, and this helps us to understand why the central policy lever to undo desegregation, since the very beginning, aimed not merely to have more choice among the publics. No, the main lever was always to divert public funds to the privates, which is where the school vouchers system comes into play, framing the educational sector as an even larger marketplace, consisting of public schools plus private schools, but with the singular, insidious goal of further concentrating wealth at the top.

How so? Typically, students are assigned to a public school based on where they live, sometimes called the school assignment area. School choice basically broadens this area to encompass more students and more public schools, thus allowing students and their parents to choose from several options. A percentage of the per-pupil spending allocation follows the student to their school of choice, thus treating schools like commodities for which students and their families shop.

Once reframed as a commodity, the logic behind school choice begs the question of why can't the funding follow students to private and religious schools as well, especially if the premise of choice is that the market will drive improvement—and, for that matter, will drive integration—whereby the bigger the market, the better the outcome. This expanded option may be in particular demand by the elite, who may not want to subsidize the education of the masses or who may not want their own children to attend schooling for and alongside the masses. School vouchers allows students to use public funds to pay for private schooling; more recent versions, sometimes called neo-vouchers, offer more indirect forms of subsidy or relief, such as tax credits for private schooling, which similarly deplete tax revenue that would otherwise be allocated to public schools.

Calls for choice, and more pointedly, vouchers, effectively reframe school funding from a social investment and a public good to a private investment and an individual commodity, a reframing credited largely to the work in the 1950s of Friedman and his students and colleagues. The rhetoric behind vouchers is that competition drives improvement, and that, as long as an industry operates like a monopoly, it is more likely to be complacent, whereas a marketplace with multiple competitors forces each one to constantly assess, innovate, and try ever harder than their peers if they are going to improve, outperform, and succeed.

Yes, competition sometimes does lead people to try harder, and yes, schools have much room for improvement, particularly the schools for the masses. *But the reality is that marketizing education, like marketizing economies, was never meant to improve the situation for the masses, and when implemented, has not succeeded at doing so. From the free-market economic reforms foisted upon struggling countries that would open up opportunities for profit out of disaster to the choice and voucher initiatives offered as means to avoid desegregation and to consolidate wealth, Neoliberal initiatives function to dismantle the public sector, to privatize as a way to fuel corporate profits, and thus, to turn the haves into have-mores.*

To this point, Friedman did not argue that vouchers would improve public education, since he was not a proponent of making the public school system more robust. Rather, he argued that vouchers were a means to an end, and that end being the privatization of public education: Where the public sector has failed to serve particular social and political interests, the private sector should be incentivized and empowered to remake the system accordingly. For Friedman, the problem was not a disinvestment in public education; the problem was public education itself, an incredibly expensive domestic enterprise that reeked of Socialism. Vouchers can be the lever that breaks up that monopoly by funneling public funds to the private schools, and while it is true that many who attend private schools are not wealthy and White, it is also true that, far and away, those who take advantage of vouchers to send children to private and religious schools tend to be wealthier Whites.

Yes, Even an Obama–Trump Convergence

When then-candidate Trump was campaigning for president in 2016, he said very little about education, except that he wanted to spend $20 billion to expand school choice, which at the time was about 30% of the federal education budget—not additional funds to be added, simply reallocated by cutting from other programs. Although his subsequent budgets never followed through on this proposal, and although he instead proposed every year to cut the overall budget, he was consistent in calling for more allocations toward the expansion of school choice, including for voucher and neo-voucher initiatives.

His first move was to nominate billionaire Betsy DeVos, a leader of school choice expansion in Michigan, to be his Secretary of Education, who was confirmed only after an historic split vote in the Senate that required the vice president to break the tie. She was confirmed in the face of a groundswell of opposition, including from over 1 million petition signatories raising concern about her lack of qualifications and her problematic track record, as well as by critics who were otherwise proponents of school choice, but who agreed that the reforms that she spearheaded in Detroit actually weakened the public school system and exacerbated inequities, particularly in the most struggling of schools.

DeVos had not taught or worked in public schools, or been a parent of public school children, or earned experience or expertise as a leader, scholar, or teacher educator in public school districts; nor was she even a supporter of candidate Trump, but to advance Trump's call to deregulate and privatize, she would be ideal. Through her family foundation—funded by the Amway fortune—and through her personal role on boards for such advocacy organizations as Jeb Bush's Foundation for Excellence in Education, she had effectively leveraged her wealth to shape policy, including the expansion of school choice and voucher programs, alongside the deregulation of charter schools, and even the expansion of the Common Core State Standards, which had been derided by Trump, but which had figured centrally in the proliferation of high-stakes testing and profiteering by the testing industry. The research had long been clear: None of these initiatives would strengthen public education overall, and instead, had already proven to indirectly or even directly exacerbate inequities—and yet these so-called reforms had been variously embraced and rejected by members of both major political parties.

In particular, the call for increased school choice, particularly in the form of expansion and deregulation of charter schools, was a hallmark of the Obama administration, including the allocation of increased federal funding for such purposes. *In fact, the Obama-era reforms aligned squarely with a number of elements of the corporate agenda for public education, best exemplified in his secretary of education Arne Duncan's School Turnaround and Reform.*

In the early 2000s, when Duncan was CEO of Chicago Public Schools, the Commercial Club of Chicago, a roundtable of business leaders, issued a report, *Left Behind*, that called for the marketizing of public schools and expansion of test-and-punish policies, and that laid the blueprint for what would, the following year, become Renaissance 2010,

Duncan's signature initiative to turn around failing schools. The reforms exacerbated inequities and fractured already struggling communities, but would soon be expanded nationwide in such initiatives as Race to the Top after Duncan sailed through confirmation in a Democratic-controlled Senate to be Obama's first Secretary of Education. His confirmation and priorities are clear signs that corporate-driven, marketizing reforms were and are not unique to Trump and DeVos, or to Republicans; this was and is a bipartisan problem.

Toward the end of Obama's second term in 2015, just before Duncan stepped down as secretary, the Nation's Report Card showed a decline in student test scores from recent years. The Council of Great City Schools issued a report documenting the extent to which students nationwide were being over-tested, not only in the number of tests, but also in the time spent on testing and test prep, with no evidence that all of the time, attention, and resources spent on testing led to any significant gains in learning or achievement. None of this was surprising; research was clear even before No Child Left Behind and Race to the Top that a testing regime would do little to improve education, and, sure enough, the result was the expanding of funding and profits for the testing industry and a narrowing of curriculum, particularly in the highest-needs schools that already showed low test scores.

Such reports cemented the consensus among Republicans and Democrats that the Obama/Duncan administration had overreached its authority and over-tested our country's schools and students with failed results. Congress seized on the timing of the long-overdue reauthorization of ESEA, as of 2015, Every Student Succeeds Act (ESSA), to advance what was long a Conservative and Republican goal: namely, to significantly weaken the federal role in education. One of the major changes in the ESSA reauthorization is a shifting of decisionmaking authority from the federal government to the states, a move that backpedals from the original reason for much of what happened in the federal era of the 1950s–1970s: to empower the federal government to push states to comply with civil rights nondiscrimination law and policy. Legislators claimed that ESSA moved away from over-testing, but such a claim was misleading: ESSA may have given states more leeway in determining the specifics, but it continued to call for annual testing and for making high-stakes decisions based on student growth, measured as gains in test scores, including evaluations of teachers and teacher preparation programs, despite the critique by researchers and test makers themselves that such use of "value-added modeling" had proven to be neither valid nor reliable for such decision-making. Over-testing, and misusing test results, continued unabated.

One of the most prominent of commonsensical ideas that still drives educational policy and reforms today is that test scores reveal all that is needed to know in order to make high-stakes decisions, from whether or not students are learning and should graduate to whether teachers are effective and should receive merit pay to whether schools should be turned around. Testing does reveal some things, like how a student answers the questions on that test, but the tests being used were never designed to direct decisionmaking in these other arenas, and with good reason: The science of testing, like all of science, is less a neutral arbiter of truths and more a tool that will always be already implicated in only certain worldviews, including standardized testing, which has origins in eugenics. Science, like any knowledge production, like all of education, cannot help but to be partial; the content and processes and frameworks of scientific inquiry cannot help but to have cultural biases; and therefore, the uses of science have always been and should always be contested.

High-stakes testing animates and embodies the Neoliberal imperative that educational effectiveness and success reflect individual responsibility and capacity and, hence, that educational improvement results from measuring performance and holding people accountable. Because Neoliberalism has become so commonsensical, so has the Neoliberal demand to test and punish, which is why both Republicans and Democrats, Conservatives and Liberals, seem to buy into that narrative and promote policies that align, failing to connect the dots of how such policies support schools to sort even more effectively. The same can be said about the bipartisan convergence around other market-based reform initiatives; from the marketizing of schools through choice, vouchers, and charter schools to the marketizing of teacher preparation via alternative, fast-track routes to certification to the marketizing of funding by moving from the federal-era focus on formula grants that targeted high needs to the focus in Race to the Top on competitive grants, which fueled privatization by requiring applicants to detail how they were going to outsource in order to spend such a large amount of money in such a short period of time.

Historicizing reforms and connecting the dots help to illuminate and rattle the ideologies and narratives that have effectively framed even what some might have thought to be the Liberal or Progressive alternatives. There are better alternatives; people just need to know where to look.

PART II

Systemic Oppression, Collective Action

I live in California now, where state officials recently announced the return of drought status, although many argued that the historic 7-year drought that supposedly ended for most parts of the state in 2019 never really ended. Regardless, the state continues to issue the most stringent restrictions of household water usage in state history. Rhetoric about the drought emphasizes less consumption: Take shorter showers, turn off the faucet when brushing teeth, wash cars less often, water lawns less frequently or not at all—and then proudly display signs on browning lawns that proclaim, "brown is beautiful"—all with the assumption that reducing household and consumer usage will make a big dent in the drought. The reality is not so simple: Of course, reducing individual and household consumption will save tons of water, but no, the dent proportionally will be small because the percentage of water consumed by individuals and households is small, at only about 5%. The business sector accounts for more than twice that.

The remaining more than 80% is used by agriculture and agribusiness with only a small slice of that taken up by small family farms. Far and away, this would include the vast commercial enterprises, particularly the large, water-intensive crops, such as almonds and rice, including rice that is exported to Asia; bottled drinking water, primarily by Nestlé; commerce-related transportation; and the biggest user of all, the cow and dairy industry, which includes the use of alfalfa, one of the most water-intensive of crops, to feed cows. We could all stop taking showers, but we would not make much of a dent in the drought, which means that the rhetorical focus on blaming individuals, on encouraging more responsible consumer behavior, detracts from the much larger problem of the system, in this case, a conglomeration of agricultural industries that are straining our natural resources.

Disciplining individuals can seem so much more graspable, more do-able than stepping back to analyze and change the larger system. Criminal justice is another helpful example. Several years ago, following the riots in

Ferguson that helped to birth the Movement for Black Lives, the FBI released a report about the criminal justice system in Ferguson. At the press conference, the FBI director explained that racial bias existed and was a result of "unconscious bias." This was an admission that, like so many other people who grew up and lived and worked surrounded by stereotypes and other racist messages, officers and officials in Ferguson internalized racial biases that, sometimes without any malintent, impacted their work. Therefore, addressing this bias was the solution.

I remember feeling pleasantly surprised that the FBI was publicly acknowledging the pervasiveness of internalized biases, but my joy quickly dissipated as I realized that the analysis of racism did not extend beyond individual bias. Reducing and attributing racism in the criminal justice system to the biases of individuals is a way to individualize the problem of racism, to scapegoat racially biased individuals, which detracts from the much larger problem of the criminal justice system as a racially biased system. Blaming racial injustice on individual bias frames the problem as outliers, as individuals-gone-bad in a temporarily broken system, as if the system is essentially good and merely needs some fixing, when in reality, the system is operating exactly as it was designed.

The so-called war on drugs further exemplifies how individualizing the problem can fortify a racist system. Many drugs are illegal to use, but in policy and practice, only certain types of drugs and only certain groups of users have been the preoccupation of this war. On the surface, it might seem benign to say that policing tends to target certain drugs more than others, but that tendency is highly racialized: Certain drugs are used more commonly in Black and Latinx urban contexts versus in predominantly White middle-class suburbs; targeting those drugs means targeting Black and Latinx communities; and once identified, poor Black and Latinx users and traffickers are more likely to face arrests and jail time than middle-class and wealthy White users and traffickers, who are more likely to face warnings or payable monetary fines. The war on drugs is less about prosecuting criminals and more about criminalizing and persecuting particular populations, thus revealing it to be a racial project; a project of racialization, of replicating racist stereotypes, of authorizing racial discrimination, all in the name of criminal justice.

The educational system is no different: The commonsensical, Neoliberal framings of any number of debates on educational reform tend to reduce the problem to the level of the individual, to blame and discipline individuals as a way to mask just how unjust the system fundamentally is. The test-and-punish regime that has dominated so-called reforms over the past 4 decades is one example, as is the marketizing of schools through choice, vouchers, and charters (described in Part I), but these are certainly not the only examples.

Part II examines several more of the biggest battles in education today, from affirmative action, free speech, and bullying, to teacher shortages and student debt. For each topic, a brief summary of the historical, social, or legal and policy contexts is offered, as is an examination of the prevailing framings and their tendency to discipline individuals while obscuring the legacy of systemic oppression. Such analyses suggest the need for a vision for education reform that is far more Progressive in its intersectional analysis, akin to aspects of New Deal and Abolitionist framings, which conclude this book as models for movement building. We begin with one of the clearest examples of Progressives stuck in Conservative, Neoliberal frames, and the potential of reframing: affirmative action.

THE CASE OF AFFIRMATIVE ACTION

The timing could not be more perfect: On the tails of losing in the 2016 *Fisher v. University of Texas at Austin* case, opponents of affirmative action argued a new case in a federal District Court, called *Students for Fair Admissions v. Harvard*. The Court ruled in Harvard's favor in 2019, but if appealed, that case may ultimately be decided by the new majority anti–affirmative action Supreme Court. The strategy almost surely to prevail? Portraying the model minority as victims in a system meant to promote diversity.

In the two previous cases about affirmative action in university admissions (1978 *Regents of University of California v. Bakke*; 2003 *Grutter v. Bollinger*), the Supreme Court consistently ruled that race can be a factor in admissions. Race is not allowed to override other factors, meaning, there cannot be racial quotas, and universities cannot reserve spots for students simply because of their race. However, race can be considered if it is merely one of several criteria, and if the university determines that campus diversity contributes positively to the educational experience of its students, particularly if it determines that the education that it offers is enhanced in a racially diverse campus. Harvard University does consider race in its whole-person review process, ranking applicants by looking at a number of factors in addition to traditional measures of ability and achievement, which for most universities today are presumed to be captured by standardized test scores and grade point averages. Previous courts referenced exactly this process, naming Harvard's as a model for the legal use of race, making it the strategic target for today's lawsuit.

In 2016, the Supreme Court affirmed these same parameters of the use of race in its *Fisher* decision. Conservative Justice Alito did not agree, and in his dissent, suggested that affirmative action might be undone if shown to discriminate not only against White applicants—which was the focus of this and previous cases—but also against applicants of color, particularly Asian American applicants. Such discrimination would refute the rationale that affirmative action contributes to diversity.

As if in anticipation of Alito's dissent, and well before the *Fisher* case concluded, the same strategist and organizer behind the *Fisher* case, Edward Blum, began recruiting Asian Americans for his newly formed Students for Fair Admissions, which would file the lawsuit against Harvard in 2014. At first glance, Asian Americans who were denied admission to Harvard seem like unlikely victims of affirmative action, given that Asian Americans are significantly overrepresented at Harvard and elsewhere: Asian Americans are approximately 5% of the U.S. population, but account for more than four times that amount at Harvard, other elite universities, and many other institutions, including community colleges.

However, for the plaintiffs, the question was never whether affirmative action led to representative enrollments, but rather, whether it prevented otherwise qualified minority applicants from getting in. Research has predicted that, if applicants for admission were evaluated solely on standardized test scores and grade point averages, then without affirmative action, undergraduate enrollments nationwide for Black and Latinx students would decrease, while for White and especially Asian American students would increase. This demographic shift is exactly what happened in California's public universities following the 1996 passage of state–ballot initiative Proposition 209 and its ban on affirmative action. Opponents point to California's resulting enrollments as proof that affirmative action discriminates, especially against Asian Americans, thus repeating a decades-old strategy of positioning Asian Americans as victims to mask what would otherwise look too clearly like White self-interest. *Victimizing Whites may not have compelled previous courts, but victimizing Asian Americans likely will, especially with the prevailing diversity rationale for affirmative action.*

President Kennedy's executive order in 1961 called for affirmative action by race in his attempt to remedy discrimination in the workforce and improve employment access and experience. In 1965, in order to address current instances of discrimination and to prevent future ones, particularly as defined by Title VII of the Civil Rights Act, the federal government created the Equal Employment Opportunity Commission. A significant distinction developed in policy and in rhetoric between equal employment opportunity and affirmative action: the former focusing on individual acts and patterns of such acts, and the latter on historical injustices and the systems and institutions that perpetuate them. Affirmative action presumed that the status quo is not and never was neutral. The status quo advantages some and discriminates against others, regardless of the intention of individuals, even in the face of the best intentions, and even when everything looks neutral, equal, and fair. Affirmative action functions not to bestow advantages in an otherwise equal playing field, but rather, to remedy the ways that some are already advantaged or disadvantaged, especially when such inequities have become so commonplace and normalized as to be unrecognized as such.

The legal rationale for affirmative action shifted in the 1978 *Bakke* case, with Justice Powell as the key swing—the same Powell whose 1971 manifesto on reversing gains of the Civil Rights Movement is often credited with inspiring the birth of the Conservative movement in the United States. Powell joined four justices to rule that racial quotas are unconstitutional, but joined with the other four justices to rule that race can be considered if it is merely one of multiple criteria and if the university in question determines that diversity contributes positively to the educational experience of its students.

The Court's rationale that considering race is allowable if in the service of building toward a diverse future departs from and is significantly narrow when compared to Kennedy's original rationale that considering race is necessary to address the historical injustices that persist, but it became and still remains the determining legal framing of affirmative action. This narrowed focus on diversity allows the continuance of historical injustices while fortifying claims that the status quo is, indeed, neutral so long as individuals play fairly. The end goal is no longer the illuminating and dismantling of systemic racism, but rather, the brewing of a more diverse and representative melting pot, which is far easier to achieve. As such, the end of affirmative action is likely to come if it can be shown to block access for some communities of color.

Students for Fair Admissions is claiming not only that Harvard's admissions process violates prior Supreme Court rulings, but also that Harvard intentionally discriminates against Asian Americans. One example offered of the anti-Asian bias in Harvard's admissions process was that reviewers consistently rated Asian American applicants lower than others on such traits as "positive personality," courage, and being widely respected. The feeling of déjà vu is uncanny: Flash back to the 1980s when Progressive Asian American groups and leaders raised concerns that personal bias and cultural insensitivity in the admissions review process at the University of California contributed directly to lowered admissions rates for Asian Americans. The university conducted an internal review and the chancellor issued an apology, but the problem of anti-Asian bias would not come to be addressed adequately. Too quickly, opponents of affirmative action seized on this controversy to conflate the two issues, mischaracterizing the problem of anti-Asian bias as evidence that affirmative action harms Asian Americans.

Even in the 1980s, the strategy to pit Asian Americans against critiques of institutional racism was not new. Back in the 1960s, media and cultural images and rhetoric began to proliferate of Asian Americans as the model minority, the model for all other minorities because, through their hard work and perseverance, they have achieved economic success, educational success, and the American Dream. In part, this image was the result of increased immigration of highly skilled labor and of international university students following the Immigration and Reform Act of 1965, as well as the result of demographic portrayals that aggregated across ethnic groups, thus masking the vastly different realities of, for instance, high-achieving descendants of East Asian and South Asian immigrants versus recent refugees from Southeast Asia, with the former far outnumbering and thereby obscuring the latter.

But perhaps the most significant reason that the stereotype of the Asian American model minority endured was the timing: At the height of the Civil Rights Movement, amid resounding claims of historical, institutional, and pervasive racism, what better counter than a racially minoritized group that was actually making it, that was doing so well as to be succeeding more than White people, or, as one news article put it, "outwhiting the Whites." The stereotype betrayed claims of structural racism: Look! There is one group of color that is making it, and maybe if all of you others would try as hard, you too could make it! Or so the thinking went.

In reality, then and now, the experiences of many Asian Americans are not captured by the model minority stereotype. Disaggregating by ethnicity, we see that the large immigrant groups that have been in the United States the longest, such as Chinese Americans, Japanese Americans, Korean Americans, and Indian Americans, have very high levels of achievement, whereas for Southeast Asian refugees and Native Hawaiians and other Pacific Islanders—who are sometimes grouped into an AAPI category—the economic and educational attainment levels are among some of the lowest of all racial groups. Even among high-achieving students, not all is well: Among college students, Asian Americans, especially Asian American young women, exhibit the highest levels of severe depression and suicide ideation.

But this definition of success that centers on narrow measures of achievement and that ignores vast in-group differences makes it easier to promulgate the Asian American model minority as the poster child of the American Dream, that humbling and hope-inspiring narrative that, through hard work and perseverance, anyone can make it. Hence, the model minority stereotype, critiqued even then as inaccurate and misleading, persisted in the public imagination because of its political salience, its reassuring implication that U.S. democracy and Capitalism are not so broken after all. It served as a powerful wedge in the 1960s, pitting one racialized group against another; it played this role again in the 1980s during the California admissions controversy; and it is playing this role again in the Harvard case, with Asian Americans on both sides: some as the face of victimization by affirmative action, and others refusing to be used in the service of White supremacy.

Polling of Asian Americans shows that a majority support affirmative action, as do the major national Asian American civil rights organizations. But some of course do not, including a coalition of 60 other Asian American organizations that filed a complaint with the Justice Department against affirmative action in the build-up to the Harvard case. My middle school classmate has long opposed affirmative action, claiming that it devalues how she, as a 1.5 generation Asian American immigrant who was teased as a nerd in school, nonetheless worked her butt off in school to get into one of the top universities, then graduate school, and eventually, obtain a six-figure management position in one of the wealthiest companies in the world. But when asked how she would change university admissions, she offered a solution that she did not realize is the whole-person review that Harvard is already doing. Misconceptions and emotions abound in the public debate about affirmative action, obscuring underlying and more fundamental questions that our society should be asking about the role of education in and for a democracy.

From Individual Deservingness to Collective Responsibility

What makes an applicant qualified or deserving of admission? Common rhetoric frames the answer in several ways: First, that universities should admit the most qualified, as if in a competition where the best wins; second, that qualification consists of ability—intelligence, talents, and capabilities—and achievement, being the accomplishments that reflect ability; third, that there are objective and consistent measures of such, like standardized test scores and GPAs; and fourth, that such measures also predict how well applicants will fit into and succeed in a given university.

Particularly when language differences and cultural differences can negatively impact whether and how a student is welcomed by other students or assessed by teachers in K–12 schools, such presumably objective measures understandably rise in importance in the minds of some Asian Americans (like my classmate) as doable steps that they can take personally to get into college in a racially hostile world.

But cultural bias exists in any assessment, including tests and grades. Any test can tell only so much about what students know, how they think and imagine, and where they flourish. Any student can be brilliant, creative, original, skillful, and inquisitive in a range of ways, and can demonstrate such capacities in equally numerous and varied ways. Not surprisingly, tests and grades can be quite unreliable in predicting how well a student will perform in college or beyond, especially when support services that were not used or available when in school are made accessible when in college. Such assessments, in other words, tell us much more about a student's prior advantages than future potential, and is precisely why, on average, students' performances on standardized tests are strongly predicted by their zip code—meaning by their family wealth and resources. Rather than assuming that affirmative action prevents the most qualified Asian Americans from getting in, how about examining how affirmative action can help to define even more broadly, accurately, and ethically the meaning of "qualified"?

What if universities were to serve a democratizing function by preparing students not merely to fit into the world as it is, but also to imagine and create the world as it could be? The capacities and potentials of applicants would be less about previous success at being the good student, and more about potential to build a more democratic future that is still in the making.

For that matter, what if universities were to serve a democratizing function by looking not only at what the individual applicant would bring or receive, but also at what the communities that the universities serve would bring or receive? This makes education less of the hyperindividualized endeavor that it is often presumed to be, and much more of the collective endeavor that it should be.

A helpful comparison would be teacher evaluations: The standard approach is to strip away all other factors to determine the value that is added by a given teacher, using something called value-added modeling, presuming that the teacher alone is what enables a student to learn. In contrast, if we take seriously the notion that "it takes a village to raise a child," and that the teacher is part of larger village or system that educates a child—along with other teachers, other school personnel, other school services and resources, classroom materials, peers, parents and other family members, guardians, community organizations, health providers, social services, the media, the libraries, mentors, elders, the arts, athletics, and so many more—then evaluating a teacher is not about removing these other factors, but rather, about considering how the teacher works synergistically with them; how the teacher contributes to, acts in concert with, and leverages that larger system.

The same is true with students. No student got to where they are, and no student will go where they will go, without all that makes up their village. Evaluating an applicant for one of the few spots for admission should not be without regard to that village. What would it mean for universities to ask how admitting this or that student would impact their village? What would it mean, in other words, for universities to take seriously their role in improving communities, in redressing historic and systemic inequities, and in advancing democracy at large, and wouldn't a refusal to hyperindividualize the applicant be a step in that direction?

Universities have a long way to go in realizing such visions, but as we broaden the scope of what universities can become, the barrier is even more clearly not affirmative action; if anything, the barrier is the Conservative rationale, and the university overall as a Conservative force, that masks the historical injustices that led here in the first place.

I was recently speaking to a former student who insisted that he supports affirmative action in principle, and that he knew the difference between affirmative action and common forms of preferential admissions—legacy admissions, being children of donors, or other considerations for diversity and distribution by major, region, type of high school, in-state versus out-of-state—but nonetheless proceeded to ask, "But, in practice, Asian Americans are disadvantaged by affirmative action, right?" He is now a medical doctor, a child of Asian immigrants, and a believer that he had to work even harder and be even smarter to get to where he is because affirmative action "worked against me."

What makes the Conservative framing of affirmative action so powerful is not merely that it detracts from the original goal of countering systemic, institutional, historic racism. No, its power lies in its ability to turn Asian Americans against ourselves with self-doubt; to inhibit solidarity between people of color by pitting Asian Americans against other communities of color; to fracture the education profession by creating false binaries between those who value diversity and those who value merit; and to derail Progressives to fight for an impoverished, perverse framing of what higher education can and should be.

THE CASE OF FREE SPEECH AND HATE SPEECH

A similar argument about surrendering to an impoverished framing of the problem can be made regarding debates about free speech and hate speech. Debates about speech have reemerged in cycles for decades, particularly in higher education. Today, this debate is magnified by one of the most, if not the most, controversial and vilified of categories of speech in higher education today: Critique of the Israeli government's violation of the human rights of Palestinians, which gets quickly mislabeled as anti-Semitic speech and, as such, quickly censored and sanctioned by both Republicans and Democrats. The mislabeling of such anti-oppressive critique as hate speech results from a failure to differentiate between, on the one hand, critically analyzing government action, and on the other, voicing hate towards people of a specific religion.

The problem here is not merely the insistence by some that anti-oppressive critique is akin to hate speech. Simultaneously, the flipside happens when insisting that instances of actual hate speech—such as the demonizing of Muslims—qualify as protected free speech, and thus, that any censuring or censoring of actual hate speech violates the speaker's First Amendment right to freedom of speech. Like the condemnation of anti-oppressive critique, the censoring of actual hate speech is sometimes accompanied by such sanctions as expulsion or termination from universities, or even criminalization; this is increasingly authorized by national leaders like Trump, who recently threatened to withhold federal funding from universities that purportedly censor free speech, or at least, the speech by those that he considered to be worthy of protection.

Whether intentional or not, three common types of arguments from both Conservatives and Liberals that are intended to protect the freedom of speech actually function to protect the right to voice hate speech, as well as to censor any criticism of hate speech. Political arguments focus on the importance of protecting controversial speech in a democracy, as when saying that everyone should be able to say what they believe; all sides should have an equal voice; all sides have the right to speak; a democracy does not censor just because the speech is unpopular. Pedagogical arguments focus on the role of speech, particularly self-disclosure, in learning, as in: All learners need to self-disclose, to put the full range of their ideas on the table, not to hold back what they are thinking and feeling. This allows for the group to then together process the opposing ideas rationally and challenge and question one another in order to learn, which therefore cannot happen if controversial ideas are censored. Ontological arguments focus on the connection between speech and authenticity:

If people cannot honestly express themselves, then they cannot be fully themselves. Underlying all three arguments is the presumption that being prevented from voicing hate and/or being forced to hear someone else critique that hate is a form of injury.

All three arguments treat all instances and forms of speech as equal, as equally warranting protection by the First Amendment, and in so doing, conflate hate speech with any and all other forms of speech, failing to distinguish the right to free speech from the protection of hate speech. One way to differentiate the two is to examine how language is used in a number of different ways, and in particular, how speech can vary in its function, meaning, and impact.

Speech can function in at least four different, yet overlapping, ways. First, speech can function as representation—that is, to represent what a person is thinking or feeling, and to capture, convey, and transmit such ideas to another person. This way of understanding language as transparent, communicative, and representational is perhaps the most common and commonsensical way of understanding the function of speech, but is certainly not the only way.

Second, speech can function as provocation, as when the speaker is trying to get a particular, or any, response from the listener(s): telling a joke to make someone laugh; emoting to evoke sympathy; saying something just to test someone, such as a flirty comment to gauge, by their reaction, the listener's romantic interest; a politically charged comment to gauge the listener's trustworthiness or affinity. These provocations can happen whether or not the initial comment is representational and conveys what the speaker actually believes.

Third, speech can function as a performance, like in theater when an actor is speaking as if someone else, as if putting on a role. Obviously this happens at Halloween or when playing charades; less obviously, this also happens in education, such as for assessments—when students take an exam or write an essay and are expressing what they believe that they are supposed to say to get an A, thus performing smartness rather than representing what they actually believe.

Fourth, speech can function as a performative, as a speech act that helps to constitute who a person is. When a baby is born and the doctor states, "It's a girl," the statement is less a description—as if the newborn already had some essential girlhood—and more a construction. The statement serves as merely the first of many ongoing, scaffolding, self-affirming acts that shape, police, and authorize that individual to become what society defines as a girl and woman physically, psychologically, culturally, socially, romantically, economically, and educationally. In this instance, by shaping the person into a particularly gendered way of being, by gendering the person, speech is constitutive.

U.S. law does recognize speech in all four of these forms. The law, for example, demands in certain instances that speech be representational—or more accurately, prohibits mis-representational speech—as when mandating that an individual cannot lie in court. The law also prohibits certain instances of speech as provocation: An individual cannot yell, "fire," in a crowded movie theater, without risk of liability for civil disturbance; and an individual cannot wage racial slurs without risk of liability for racial harassment. The law protects certain instances of speech as performance, such as the fictional self-representations of undercover officers, or whistleblowing anonymously or otherwise, though this form of speech is less and less protected these days, especially within the public sector. And the law recognizes the constituting function of certain instances of speech as performatives; this can be in the affirmative, like when an officiant pronounces two people to be married, or in the negative, like when the decision not to self-disclose as gay means that an individual has not yet been constituted as gay, and therefore, can serve in a military that prohibits gay people from serving. This convoluted logic was encapsulated in the Clinton administration's Don't Ask, Don't Tell policy that hinged on self-disclosing as the only constitutive act that counts, at least, per the gaze of the military.

Where the law falls short is its presumption that the speaker originates the harm that can result from speech and, in particular, that the speaker bears responsibility for wielding speech to injure. But the meaning and impact of speech does not originate from the speaker, which becomes clearer when examining how context matters.

From Individual Acts to Power Relations

Speech can vary in meaning depending on the context in which it is used. When I was in high school, my friends and I sometimes used the word *bad* to mean *good*, like if we went to see a movie and really liked it, and someone asked us about the movie, we might have said, "oh, that movie was baaaad," meaning, the movie was really good. Words or phrases do not have essential meanings that stay consistent regardless of context, as if meanings are embedded in what results from sequencing several letters or characters or sounds together. That is not how language works.

Rather, words and phrases have meaning because they cite particular discursive histories, they cite how that word or phrase has been used over time within a particular community, which is why, at different times or in different communities, the same word can mean different things. I might tell a friend that a movie that I loved was *bad*—meaning good—and then say that the book that we read in class and that I hated was *bad*—meaning unenjoyable. Even in the same historical moment, the same cultural context, and the same geographic location, the same word can have different meanings because each iteration cites different discursive histories and conjures a different pattern of how that word has been used within and by a given group.

The listener can understand, if and when their reading of a given iteration is the same as that of the speaker. The meaning and impact depend not only on the intent of the speaker, but also the understanding of the listener; the listener is always reading and interpreting the speech in ways that the speaker may anticipate, but can never control and may never fully know. This is why misinterpretation and unintended injury happen all the time. I might think that calling a movie bad when speaking to my friends will be interpreted as good, but some might think it strange that I seem pleased while negating the movie, or think that I was trying to be ironic when I was not.

This situation crops up in education as well. If I were still a K–12 teacher, I might think that coming out as LGBTQIA+ will position me as a role model, resulting in younger LGBTQIA+ students feeling more comfortable with themselves. It is also possible, however, that some students might pull back from me out of fear that associating with me will reveal that they, too, have been in the closet, resulting in feeling less comfortable with themselves and with me. The speech act of coming out can be empowering to some, but fear-invoking to others, even if they are all LGBTQIA+, and even if they are all understanding the history that I am citing. This happens because they are all looking through different lenses; they are all listening through different filters.

Just as the meaning can vary, so too can the emotional, political, and moral impact—be it empowering, entertaining, hurtful, denigrating—depending on the discursive histories and the power relations that are cited and read in that moment. For example, the phrase "that's so gay" is often used as a negative characterization or interpersonal jab, like if someone does not like a television show, they might say that that show was "so gay," or if someone wants to insult a peer, they might say, "You're so gay." The listener will likely understand that the speaker does not like the show or the person because that phrase cites how gayness is often understood to be something bad and, perhaps more significantly for the latter, is often a tool used to push others down. But in different contexts, such as if someone is gay and is surrounded by other gay people, the phrase "that's so gay" can be a very humorous and playful thing. For example, if one of my queer friends is admiring the colorful aloha shirt I am wearing, they might say, "That shirt is so gay," intended fully as a compliment, citing how gayness can be affirming in affinity groups, or how reclaiming points of difference can be a source of strength.

Hierarchies and power relations exist in the discursive histories being cited—such as the history of the military using gayness as a reason to discriminate. Hierarchies and power relations also exist in the speech event—such as the moment when the speaker is bullying the listener. Both sets of power relations can influence how the words or phrases impact the listener. When a speech act cites, say, the history of certain words being used in the service of White supremacy, all of that oppressive history gets encoded into the words, thus turning the act of speaking into an act that now leverages all that hate in the service of the intended impact. In such an instance, if spoken with the purpose, whether intentional or not, to perpetuate racial discrimination in the moment being spoken, especially if by a White person against a person of color, the power relations embedded in the cited history plus the power relations enacted between speaker and listener turn the speech event into a forceful embodiment or manifestation of White supremacy in play.

Speech always implicates power. This is why speech, especially hate speech, can be so injurious, so much more destructive than merely the hateful intent of the speaker. *All of these things can influence the meaning and impact of language: The discursive histories, the power relations, the particularities of the speech event, the delivery by the speaker, and the lenses of the listener. Clearly, not all speech is equal. Some speech can cause far more harm whereas other speech can be far more in need of protection and amplification, depending on what histories are being cited or built on and what power relations are being reinforced or challenged.*

U.S. law does recognize that words can wound, can injure, which is the basis of the prohibition of hate speech, but where law falls short is in misattributing where the harmfulness of hate speech originates; what or who is responsible for the harm? By presuming that words are the weapons that can afflict harm, and that the speaker is using words like weapons, the focus of law becomes either silencing or censoring certain speech to prevent harm from occurring in the first place, or punishing the speaker for speech and harm that have occurred, rather than tackling the power relations and the oppressive histories being cited.

Universities have increasingly become ground zero for the battle over hate speech, with rhetoric around academic freedom as the device of choice to protect hate speech. So long as rhetoric about free speech centers on benign political, pedagogical, and ontological arguments and on the hyperindividualized framing of what gives speech the power to injure, and so long as a muddled, impoverished definition of what constitutes academic freedom prevails, hate speech will continue to be indistinguishable from the forms of speech that warrant protection. Like U.S. law, universities tend to focus on speech as individual acts and on harm as originating from the speaker, which is a hyperindividualized framing that ultimately reinforces arguments to protect hate speech.

Reframing the debate on free speech requires reframing the central arguments about why such protections are needed. Pedagogically, it is not the case that all speech needs to be aired in order for learning to happen, because hate speech can serve to curtail learning: It can injure others in the room, it can re-enact the very forms of oppression being cited, thus silencing all who are implicated in that citing, preventing all from the collective deliberating inquiry that even the defenders of hate speech articulate as a prerequisite for learning.

The same is true with political arguments. It is not the case that all sides must have equal voice in order for democracy to thrive, because democracy is not only about voicing diverse ideas. No, it is also about collectively deliberating those ideas, which cannot and should not be attempted without the prerequisite that each participant hold themselves accountable for examining and challenging the ways that any speech, including their own, can draw on discursive histories and power relations in ways that injure, that oppress, that run counter to democracy.

The purpose of protecting the freedom of speech in a democracy should be to protect the freedom to question and challenge the oppressive histories and power relations that prevent the realization of democracy, not simply the allowance of anyone to say anything without any accountability for what results. Debates about protecting free speech that fail to examine the impact of hate on learning and on democracy will service the very oppressions that such protections purport to counter.

THE CASE OF BULLYING AND VIOLENCE

A similar analysis can be made of attempts to address bullying. As with attempts to counter hate speech, antibullying policies and programs commonly rest on the presumption that the harmful act, be it hate speech or bullying, is like a weapon; it is presumed that the perpetrator is wielding that weapon to injure, is choosing to act in ways that injure, and therefore, that reducing bullying requires both disciplining the perpetrator after the act and discouraging such acts in the first place. Some antibully-ing policies and programs aim to constrain or contain the potential bully in order to discourage bullying, such as through explicit classroom rules and norms, or increased adult presence and other forms of surveillance. Others aim to punish the bully after bullying occurs by taking away privi-leges, suspending from school, and increasingly, criminalizing through involvement of the juvenile justice system as punishment or deterrent. Still others aim to improve interpersonal relationships between perpetra-tor and target, improve school climate, and alleviate emotional trauma after bullying occurs via restorative justice and healing circles.

Clearly, some of these methods of disciplining bullies are not always intended to be punitive. They, too, can be reparative, as they aim to teach or support the student to become a better student, or better citizen of the school, or better community member. But such a goal can be an ironic one, given that the narrow definition of the good student or good child might have been an ideal that the bully failed to achieve—not because they could not, but because they refused to—which makes such inter-ventions akin to the assimilative demand that drove bullying in the first place. In this way, disciplining might stop bullying temporarily, but is fundamentally a repressive act, not a liberatory or even pedagogical one. Yes, both the bully and the bullied—and the bystanders—need healing and growth, but that cannot be the only or even the primary strategy.

The narrowed, hyperindividualized focus on disciplining the bully is a scapegoating method that detracts from the much larger system, particularly the political, cultural, and community contexts, including familial and peer relations, that drove the bullying in the first place. It may appear that bullies are simply mean or evil, but such an interpretation would be miss-ing the bigger picture. Similarly, it is simplistic to presume that bullies act out merely because of their own psychological and emotional struggles, which undoubtedly has some truth to it, but such a framing fails to take one more step back to ask where the psychological and emotional strug-gles originated. For that question, the queering of normalcy proves vital.

School bullies are most often boys, which raises the question, "What are the prevailing stories in society about what it means to be a boy or a man?" Hegemonic or dominant forms of masculinity are not something that a person just has or is; rather, it is an ideal, something that a person must constantly pursue, animate, claim, and prove to others in order to self-ascribe and be read by others as masculine in the moment, or more accurately, as masculine in-the-making. This happens less in the affirma-tive than in the negative. Instead of showing masculine traits, it is done by disproving the antithesis, by disproving that a person is not-masculine, by distancing oneself from anything that might be deemed feminine, or queer, or culturally deficient, or weak. This imperative to constantly disprove helps to reveal the fragility of toxic forms of masculinity, the inability to ever permanently be, and the exhaustive efforts required to pursue, only to fail and have to pursue again. The toxic masculinities that pervade the United States today require an ongoing display of ontological distance from and social superiority to their Other. Unsurprisingly, toxic masculinities both reinforce and rely on misogyny, homophobia, transphobia, racism (even if a person is not White), and their intersection, manifesting even among queer men, men of color, and other men on the margins when internalized.

Where the hate, bullying, and violence become particularly acute and demonstrative is where the proving of masculinity requires the policing of fine lines. There is a fine line, for example, between showing the emotional vulnerability in a heterosexual relationship that is required in order to deepen an emotional connection and showing emotionality or weakness that crosses the line into being perceived as too feminine. There is a fine line between showing homoerotic comradery or guy-play in locker rooms and in drunken stupor when nudity, sexualized touch, and flirtatiousness are humorous and teasing, and showing attraction and desire that crosses the line into being or doing something that will be deemed too gay. In both instances, it is not surprising that violence is often sexual in nature— the rape of women or the bashing of genitals of other men—since it is at the junctures of sexual meaning-making where policing is most at stake.

In these ways, bullying operates through several dualities: It pushes some up, serving a protective function by bestowing certain social and psychological benefits, but also pushes some down as a way to police the fragile, contingent categories on which social norms and hierarchies hinge. It constitutes the actor who is constantly presenting himself akin to the ideals of toxic masculinity, but it also constitutes all those being Othered as the foils of that claim. It operates through the violence that the actor directs toward the Other, but also can incite violence as backlash, as when the Other further polices those lines, such as when internalizing the hate or fighting back. Disciplining the bully typically addresses only one side of these dualities, but perhaps not surprisingly, it is often the other sides in which society is most invested.

Of course, boys are not the only ones enacting bullying, and bullying and ostracism do not only happen in person. The widespread epidemic of girls bullying and the rapidly growing epidemic of bullying online or cyberbullying both hinge on other forms of normalcy and identity formation, and thus, operate in ways both similar to and different than traditional bullying. Furthermore, every school and community has different structural and cultural elements, different norms, different problems; there are different dots that need to be connected in order to understand bullying in any specific context, and that is where local expertise and knowledge likely shape this analysis in ways that refuse standardized solutions.

Yet another contributing factor of bullying is the normalizing of violence that manifests in both a culture of violence and cycles of violence. Perpetrators of bullying are very likely to have been bullied or to still be bullied, and therefore, punishment and threat may be effective only at momentarily curtailing some actions. The underlying trauma that was never addressed or the violence that continues to traumatize in homes, communities, and the world remains unchanged as primary drivers of cyclical violence that may erupt later on in ever worse ways. This is especially so when political and cultural contexts authorize and fuel such violence, like with the increasingly frequent and vociferous attacks from public officials and media personalities toward Muslims, refugees, transgender people, people with disabilities, people who are overweight or larger bodied, and other similarly marginalized peoples and communities.

Even schools enact violence, or are spaces where authorized violence occurs, be that physically, in the form of a security officer beating a child or diagnoses that demand unnecessary medicalization; culturally, through the demeaning of certain groups in the curriculum or exclusion of certain groups from parental involvement; or various other subtle and overt ways. Bullying between individuals is, in some ways, a microcosm of that larger arena, and given the many ways that schools authorize violence, bullying is just one more of the technologies through which schools sort.

From Disciplining Actors to Transforming Systems

In recent years, another form of violence has received renewed attention nationally: mass shootings on school grounds, reminiscent of the 1990s when a similar series of mass shootings gripped the county. Even then, several patterns emerged that magnified the injurious effect of normative masculinity and normalized cyclical violence: The perpetrators were often bullied, harassed, and ostracized prior to shooting. They were bullied, not merely as social outcasts, but through the use of homophobic language—"you're a fag"—even if they did not self-identify as gay: This is not uncommon, given how the two most common ways that children and teens tease one another these days is to use language of being "fat" or a "fag," whether or not the targets are overweight or LGBTQIA+.

For many of the perpetrators, there was not only failed integration and social ostracism as contributing factors, but also a failed sense of success romantically; there was a sense of failed heteronormative masculinity for these teens who, almost exclusively, were White boys who expressed attraction to girls. Racial harassment sometimes intersected as well: In one instance of a mass shooting on a university campus, the shooter was a male student of color who complained of enduring not only sexual rejection, but also racial epithets.

Almost all of the shooters were steeped in cultures of paramilitarism and gun violence, using the Internet to research guns and warfare, militias, and armed conflict. On these sites, violence was celebrated as a solution to problems, particularly problems with societal institutions, or their place in society, or, at least, how others in society treat them. At the time, the pattern of school shootings dominated the media, as did stories involving bombs, such as the Oklahoma City bombing and the capture of the serial bomber known as the Unabomber.

Today's mass shootings on school grounds are similarly occurring at a time when mass shootings outside of schools are dominating the news, like in shopping malls, religious buildings, and nightclubs. General mass shootings sit at a similarly complex intersection of factors, including that, overall, male shooters are more likely than not to have been perpetrators of domestic violence, and in turn, that perpetrators of domestic violence are more likely than not to have been or currently be serving in the military, on the police force, or some combination thereof. This is not to say that people in the military or police are naturally more violent, but rather that there is a culture of militarism and policing that cannot be disentangled from the view that violence is a solution to our problems. Recent laws authorize the use of guns and violence, such as "stand your ground" laws that allow the use of guns for self-protection, as does widespread state-sanctioned violence, such as through militarized policing that particularly target Black communities, and to which the Movement for Black Lives emerged in response.

All of this happens alongside violence-saturated media, entertainment, and cultures, shaping not only the legality of violence, but also the gut feeling for many people that violence is the solution. *To simply prevent access to guns or punish and lock up the perpetrators will not get at the roots of the problem; things like the laws and institutional norms, cultural narratives and resources, and misogynist and racist ideologies that permeate and endure in our society need to be addressed.*

Reframing from disciplining individuals to transforming systems requires connecting the dots, and therefore, the media play a large role in shaping the public's understanding or misunderstanding of the issues at stake. Then and now, coverage of mass shootings serves to racialize who counts as tragic. For the most part, the mass shootings that captured the country's attention 20 years ago were tragedies that occurred in middle-class White suburbs, and the lack of analysis or even acknowledgment of this context promulgated not only a partial, racialized media coverage of school-ground violence, but also a partial, racialized understanding of the problem of violence itself. Critics of the media coverage noted that the media was suggesting or implying that this level of violence was not happening before and is not happening elsewhere.

But that is not the case. There may not have been a cluster of mass shootings with large numbers of deaths and injuries per instance elsewhere, but appallingly high rates of violence and trauma, including from gun violence, have long been occurring on and around school grounds in, for instance, Black and Latinx communities in urban contexts. What warrants media attention and national outrage? Why aren't other forms of school-ground violence receiving the same level of outrage and attention? What racist stereotypes are normalizing or dismissing the violence enacted on young Black and Latinx children? Race and social class intersect with all of these issues, shaping what counts as a tragedy, and who counts as innocent and deserving of protection. Addressing the larger problem requires telling a much more complex story.

THE CASE OF TEACHER SHORTAGES

When I was a university professor, whether teaching education or ethnic studies, I often began my courses by watching and discussing Nigerian novelist Chimamanda Adichie's TED Talk "The Danger of a Single Story," describing how any person, any group, any culture or country will always have multiple, competing stories about who they are and should be. Given that every story cannot help but to be partial, to reflect only certain perspectives and experiences, to serve only certain political interests and social functions, and perhaps even more importantly, given that only certain stories seem to count as commonsensical, as dominant, as worthy of repetition or somehow authorized as more true, there is a danger of buying into any single story as *the* story.

As important as asking for counterstories is, it is equally important to ask about what role the single story plays socially, politically, and ideologically in this moment. Single stories about racialized groups often consist of stereotypes that reinforce White supremacy, which might make the danger of such stories more easily apparent. But for certain stories, the danger can be more insidiously hidden within.

Across the country today, many states and districts are telling stories of a teacher shortage, with salary as one big contributing factor. For example, in Hawai'i, where I grew up, the Hawai'i Scholars for Education and Social Justice (HSESJ) points out that, when adjusted for cost of living, teachers there are the lowest paid in the nation. Not surprisingly, roughly 1,000 teachers leave their positions in Hawai'i public schools each year, and these numbers appear to be rising, which means that annually, the schools must hire 10% or more of the teacher workforce. At the start of the 2018–2019 school year, 1,029 of the 14,437 Hawai'i teacher positions were either filled with unlicensed or emergency-hire teachers (49.4%) or left vacant (50.6%). With a nearly equal number of these cases in elementary and high schools, the shortage can affect more than 60,000 students, or one-third of the student population.

In California, where I now live, the California Alliance of Researchers for Equity in Education (CARE-ED) point out that the statewide student–teacher ratio is the highest in the nation, at 24:1, compared to the national average of 16:1, although in large urban districts across the state, those ratios are unevenly distributed, with some classes over 36:1. California would need to hire 135,000 teachers just to equal the national average, but only for now, because the ongoing wave of retirements will significantly increase the shortage: 34% of teachers are aged 50 and older, and 10% of teachers are 60 and older. Nationwide, teacher attrition is especially high in poor, urban schools, where on average about one-fifth of the entire faculty leaves annually, which is roughly 50% higher than the rate in more affluent schools.

The pipeline does not give much hope: In the last decade, enrollment in teacher-education programs statewide dropped by 75%, and consequently, the number of newly credentialed teachers annually has steadily declined, consistently falling far short of the number of vacancies, resulting in a dramatic increase in the issuance of substandard credentials and permits. In 2015–2016, California issued more than 10,000 intern credentials, permits, and waivers to individuals who had not completed—or sometimes not even started—preparation to be the teacher of record, which is more than double the number issued in 2012–2013, and which is close to the number of full credentials issued.

These trends negatively impact some groups more than others. By far, the schools most impacted by this compromised teaching force are the ones serving predominantly students of color, Indigenous students, immigrant and refugee students, and students in high-poverty areas, as well as students in high-needs fields like special education and bilingual education.

A few years ago, I was interviewed for a local television news program in San Francisco on the teacher shortage. For that fall, schools statewide needed to hire 14,000 teachers, and San Francisco alone needed 500. Before the taping began, the reporter described that he was also looking for current or recently departed teachers who could speak to the unaffordability of living on a teacher salary, and asked me if I thought that the high cost of living in San Francisco was the primary reason for the shortage. I replied that, yes, the low teacher salaries compared to the high cost of living was indeed a significant contributing factor, but that the shortage was caused by a number of factors and made for a much more complicated story. In my 20-minute interview, I tried to explain some of the other factors, only to watch the segment that evening and see myself quoted for only half a sentence about how the high cost of living drives the shortage!

From Single Stories to Intersectional Analyses

Teachers do need higher salaries. One of the most salient and heart-breaking stories to emerge from the wildcat teacher strikes in the spring of 2018 that stopped business as usual in six right-to-work states—particularly in states with some of the lowest salaries in the country—was how common it was for teachers to work a second, and a third, and even a fourth job to make ends meet, as well as to subsidize the budget for class-room materials out of pocket because the schools were so underfunded. But to then equate the shortage with low salaries runs a risk: While it could justify allocating more funds to increase salary, it could also justify seeking a pool of prospective teachers who would be willing to work for lower salaries because they have no plans to make teaching their long-term career. This is exactly what was observed in San Francisco when some proposed reserving a potentially growing number of slots for Teach for America as a way to build a more reliable and expandable pipeline.

In my interview, I tried to tell multiple stories in order to paint a more complex picture. The crisis is not everywhere; many districts do not have shortages. Shortages are not new, particularly in urban and rural areas, in poorer areas, and in fields like special education, bilingual education, and STEM, which have all long struggled to recruit and retain. Across the country, districts had been bracing for a large wave of retirements as the baby boomer population aged over the past 2 decades. In California, just as this retirement wave began, districts were terminating thousands of teachers because of budget constraints. The pipeline into the teaching profession is shrinking as enrollments in teacher-preparation programs plummet. The pipeline into higher education in general is shrinking because, nationwide over the next few years, the sheer number of college-aged students will be shrinking; not the high school graduation rate, but the population itself.

The wave of so-called reforms that restrict and punish teachers are deprofessionalizing teaching, disempowering and demoralizing them, and making it more and more difficult to teach; this is perhaps the biggest reason that I hear from former teachers for why they left the profession. Some of the so-called solutions to the shortage are exacerbating the problem, such as replacing teachers who taught for 2 or 3 decades with teachers who plan to teach for only 2 or 3 years, accelerating the revolving door.

As made clear from the teacher strikes, the salaries are often unlivable, and some teachers work additional jobs to make ends meet. In San Francisco, the cost of living, particularly the cost of housing, is simply out of reach, and continues to rise with gentrification and the investment-property boom, including a growing number of private properties used only for Airbnb rentals. Some teachers are forced to find homes outside the city in more affordable neighborhoods and then deal with the commute times that have increased significantly over the past few years, thanks largely to the flood of drivers for the rideshare companies, Uber and Lyft.

Regardless of the number of teachers needed, the crisis also hinges on the demographics of teachers needed: The teaching profession has long been around 80% White women, similarly for the teacher-education profession, despite decades of efforts to diversify both. The mandating of more and more high-stakes entrance exams and performance assessments that purportedly, but do not, raise the so-called bar of who is going into teaching are contributing to the Whitening of the teaching profession.

Thus, the story of the teacher shortage is a multifaceted one of demographic changes, problematic reforms, attacks on labor, corporate greed, gentrification, deprofessionalizing of teaching and demonizing of teachers, Neoliberalism, Colonialism, racism, heteropatriarchy; the list goes on. By focusing on only a single story, it is impossible to understand the problem fully, to address the range of factors that contribute, just as it is far more likely to adopt a solution that may sound commonsensical but serves the interests of those who already benefit from the conditions of this crisis in the first place. This exacerbates the crisis, which justifies more corporate intervention, and the cycle self-perpetuates.

THE CASE OF STUDENT DEBT

The tendencies to seek, offer, and default to single stories, to simple and simplistic solutions, abound in education. In the fall of 2019, several Democratic candidates for U.S. president put forth proposals for addressing the $1.6 trillion in higher-education student-loan debt that affected about 45 million people nationwide. On average, the debt per person was in the $20,000 range at the undergraduate level, and in the $30,000 range at the masters level; this included a staggering number of individuals who never completed their degree programs because, even with loans and even if working while attending college or university, they could not afford to continue. Currently, only a little over half of all matriculated students complete their 4-year undergraduate programs within 4 to 6 years, and of those, two-thirds leave with debt.

The student debt crisis is a recent phenomenon. Half a century ago, tuition was a fraction of what it is now at colleges and universities across the country, even when adjusting for inflation, and the vast majority of students receiving financial aid were receiving need-based scholarships and grants. But in the time since, tuition has skyrocketed and, without a similar expansion of funding for need-based scholarships and grants, students without family wealth were turning in increasing numbers to increasingly large loans, at the elite private schools, but also at public institutions.

Over the past 3 decades, public institutions have experienced a drastic reduction in the percentage of their operating budgets that came from tax dollars—in some institutions, dropping from over 40% to under 20%—forcing institutions to increase tuition to make up for the lost revenue. Today, across all institutions, the percentage of financial need being met by grants and scholarships is a fraction of what it used to be and, not surprisingly, the cumulative student debt has doubled in size from just 20 years ago. Students of color, working-class students, and first-generation students are far more likely to attend public institutions than private ones, and far more likely to be the ones in debt.

Student loans can come in the form of public loans, which are the federal guaranteed student loans, as well as from a growing body of private loans. *Both types are vastly underregulated, thanks to 4 decades of advocacy by lenders to deregulate and, perhaps more significantly, to exempt student loan borrowers from bankruptcy protection. A 2005 legislation, championed by Democratic then-senator and 2020 presidential candidate Joe Biden, prevented about $150 billion in private loans from being discharged, effectively enabling the student loan industry to epitomize fraud and predatory lending.*

Lenders of student loans can and do manipulate the terms of the loan quite easily compared to other types of loans, particularly in cases of default. The failure to make a regularly scheduled payment is a loan delinquency, and delinquency over time can become a loan default—a failure to meet the terms of the loan—and within the student loan industry, the conditions to avoid elevating to default status are typically stringent, and the consequences of default disproportionate. Lenders can quickly categorize a borrower as defaulted, thus authorizing penalties in the form of additional fees of hundreds or thousands of dollars added to the principal, as well as increases in the interest rate by several percentage points, instantly jacking up what began in the single digits, with 7–8% APR commonly the starting rate, to an APR in the double digits; these have compounding effects that are staggering.

A housing loan is a helpful contrast: On a 30-year fixed-rate mortgage, a borrower might end up paying two or three times the amount of the initial principal because of compounding interest. But for a student loan that has suffered added penalties and increased interest rates, the borrower can end up owing more than four to five times the amount of the initial principal, with monthly payments far exceeding what was initially anticipated and affordable at the start. The borrower is now even less able to pay back, particularly if the borrower lacks family wealth, did not complete the degree program that presumably would have resulted in a higher-paying job, took a temporary break from enrolling in classes that triggered early repayment, or simply does not earn a high enough income to begin repayment while still a student.

The default rate for student loans is high compared to that for other types of loans, which is perhaps not surprising, given that for many other types of loans—home, car, business—some combination of assets and income are needed to get approval in the first place, whereas for student loans, the assumption is that such capacity simply does not exist yet, but will in due time. Some borrowers default while they are still students: Whereas public loans typically defer repayment until after leaving higher education—and can defer even further or reduce the principal under certain conditions, like teaching in a high-needs area immediately after graduation—private loans commonly require that repayment begins almost immediately and while still a student. This may have been possible initially, but is likely impractical if life circumstances change with conditions like unanticipated expenses or loss or reduction of income.

To make matters worse, there is no reprieve if unable to pay: Riding the wave of deregulation in the 1990s and early 2000s that ballooned the subprime mortgage industry—an industry that, a few years later, would collapse and instigate a global financial crisis and recession—and capitalizing on the Neoliberal framing of education as a commodity that was also in full force by the early 2000s, was the successful lobbying by lenders for the 2005 legislation that would exempt student loans from bankruptcy protection. Normally, in the case of bankruptcy, a personal or business loan can be discharged, but this is not so for student loans: Even after declaring bankruptcy, the borrower remains responsible for repayment. Once in default, lenders gain authority to seize other income and assets, including financial assistance that is intended to support individuals and families in times of hardship, like unemployment income, Social Security, and even public loans and grants that result from disasters, such as hurricane destruction of their homes.

Student loans are exempt from bankruptcy protections—the same loans to which lenders attach steep penalties and increases in interest rates unlike those for any other types of loans; the same loans that face some of the highest rates of default among all types of loans; the same loans taken out by individuals who were already struggling financially but sought the loans to better their lives through education. The terms from the start were predatory, and the rippling effect after is profoundly debilitating: Ballooning debt and defaulting on loans negatively impact the borrower's credit history, their employment opportunities, their livelihood and the livelihood of their families, as well as the assets of anyone who may have cosigned their loans. In so doing, this lessens the capacity of everyone within this larger circle from contributing to the economy. *The student debt crisis causes the have-nots to have even less, providing just another example of the sorting function of the U.S. educational system.*

Of the 2020 Democratic presidential candidates' proposals for addressing this debt, the most ambitious and expensive came from Bernie Sanders, who was the only to call for forgiving the entire aggregate debt. His position sparked debates about whether the blanket forgiveness is fair to those who successfully repaid or can afford to repay, as well as whether the federal government can afford to do so even if it wanted to. In response, the Sanders campaign did more than show the fairness and affordability of such a proposal by doubling down, reminding voters of what he had been proposing for years: an even more ambitious proposal of free tuition for public higher education. Although debates and media coverage tended to fixate on questions of the cost of debt forgiveness, the Sanders campaign was asking a different set of questions—questions of priorities.

Budgets and policies should reflect priorities and values. Despite calls for austerity, the reality is that the federal government spends more than ever before—and more than its rivals combined—on its military–industrial complex and war industry. Just a few years ago, the federal government bailed out the banks and financial institutions at several times the level of the student debt, effectively making the banks and bank executives and investors vastly richer while the masses who lost home equity and savings saw next to nothing trickle down. The United States has far more than the $1.6 trillion needed to forgive student debt—after all, it came up with several times that amount for its 2020 COVID-19 stimulus packages—and would simply need to choose to allocate funds in ways that reflect its priorities, if education and the poor were, indeed, priorities.

Furthermore, the United States would have far more revenue to begin with if it were to fairly tax wealthy individuals and corporations, which it does not. The very wealthy are grossly undertaxed, thanks to loopholes that make the tax system even more regressive—where the wealthy ultimately pay a lower percentage of their income and wealth than the poor do. Some of the wealthiest are getting away with paying absolutely nothing. In 2018, for example, Amazon made over $11 billion in profits, but paid $0 in taxes. That same year, 60 corporations made a combined $79 billion in profits, but paid $0 in taxes, instead receiving $4.3 billion in rebates; the federal government gave them money instead of receiving anything from them. One way that the wealthiest have avoided paying taxes is by keeping what is now $15 trillion of U.S. wealth in shell companies in offshore tax havens. The U.S. tax system enables the wealthy to get even wealthier.

Higher education is no different: Those who have can get even more. The student debt crisis exposed how the U.S. higher education system and the related loan industry work synergistically to make the poor even poorer, but the flipside is true as well. The 2019 college admissions bribery scandal exposed how dozens of wealthy parents, including celebrities and business leaders, paid or bribed intermediaries to help to get their children accepted to top universities. The scandal served as a reminder that such blatant leveraging of wealth is only the tip of a vastly larger iceberg of ways that the wealthy and elite game the system to advantage their children.

The transactions can be directly with universities, as when making donations, be they monetary or in kind. But transactions can also involve a host of other players that make the pipeline into elite institutions more likely. Some parents send their children to elite K–12 schools—be they selective private schools or prestigious public schools located in wealthier neighborhoods—that serve as funnels to the top universities. Some parents provide the resources for any number of experiences that prepare them to compete for admission—from extracurricular activities to tutors to simply the freedom from obligations outside of school that help to support the family, like working part-time or babysitting siblings. U.S. law might guarantee access to a public K–12 school, but not access to a college or university, and in the marketplace that is higher education, the influence of wealth is no different than in any other industry.

The call, then, for free tuition at public colleges and universities disrupts the marketization of education, framing it not as a commodity, affordable only to some, but as a fundamental right to be paid for by all and accessible to all. Sanders called for more fairly taxing the wealthy in order to relieve student debt; but it is the reframing of education as a right, the elevating of education as a budget priority, that is the far bigger investment both financially and ideologically.

From Commodity to Public Good

Critics call Sanders's proposals Socialist, but the proposals are not anywhere near as Socialist as they could or should be. Medicare for All is a helpful comparison of a proposal criticized for sounding too Socialist, even though it is far from it. Yes, Medicare for All would make public the health insurance system, turning it into what is called a single payer system, but what it would not do is make public the much larger healthcare system, which means that the government would not take over hospitals, doctors would not become government employees, and other features that would constitute socialized medicine. Medicare for All would change how people access and pay for healthcare, moving the financial burden from the individual to the collective, thus making the responsibility for paying for healthcare a collective responsibility, calling for people to look after each other; everyone invests because it makes everyone better off, rather than an individual model where each person is on their own. However, the healthcare industry itself would remain mostly private, as it currently is, albeit with more regulation. Medicare for All is a far cry from making the much larger healthcare system into a public industry and healthcare itself into a public good, but is a step towards that.

The same is true with student debt relief. Although expensive, it is nonetheless a one-time, short-term remedy for the past and current harm enacted by predatory lending that does not address the sorting function of higher education. The more ambitious proposal of free tuition for public colleges and universities makes higher education accessible now and in the future by moving the financial burden from the individual to the collective, but even that is a limited solution that sits parallel to Medicare for All: Both treat financial access to an enterprise—versus the enterprise itself—as a collective responsibility. Free tuition applies only to public colleges and universities, whereas Medicare for All applies in principle to both public and private healthcare providers. That is a key difference, but a key similarity is that the government is not proposing to make all of higher education, or all of healthcare, a public industry. Free tuition is not socialized education, and debt relief is even less so.

A hint at what it would mean to socialize education, to treat it as a public good rather than a commodity, is to consider another of Sanders's proposals, articulated during the Black and Brown Democratic Presidential Forum in 2019. When criticizing the country's dependency on local property taxes to fund public schools, he proposed instead that the United States needs "to make sure the federal government plays an active role to make sure that those schools who need it the most get the funds that they deserve." In contrast to the 2015 reauthorization of the ESEA that weakened the federal government by delegating much decisionmaking authority to the states, *Sanders proposed that the federal government play an even more impactful role than in the past: Not only leveraging funds to push states to comply with nondiscrimination law, but also federalizing school funding, pooling funding nationally and then redistributing with an eye toward equity.*

Currently, school funding consists primarily of state and local funding and, on average, we see that in poorer communities, individuals are paying a greater percentage of their income in state and local taxes but seeing a much lower amount of per-pupil spending when compared with wealthier communities; ballot initiatives have failed to change these regressive formulas. Wealthier communities can be spending several times the amount per pupil that poorer communities are spending. Federal policies and programs have exacerbated these inequities, including competitive grant programs that fueled privatization such as Race to the Top, and funding contingencies that were tied to so-called reforms that do not work, such as high-stakes testing—all of which were and are making schools less effective and less democratic.

Inequitable funding is a primary driver of educational disparities and will continue to plague U.S. schools so long as the primary source of funding is local property taxes. Increasing funding for struggling schools has proven to increase student learning and students' future economic prosperity. This was Sanders's target: By federalizing school funding, the educational system becomes a more collective, national responsibility. But such goals never got much attention, within the Democratic party or otherwise, because as has happened several times before, in the 1940s, the 1970s, and the 1990s, Communist-baiting and Socialist-baiting of such ideas and of Sanders himself proved effective in instigating a retreat by the Left and a continued insistence, at least within the mainstream Democratic party, to focus on how to help individuals to succeed in the system rather than to fundamentally change the system.

Sanders and others are right to point out that the rich decry Socialism for the poor but have no problems benefiting from Socialism for the rich. The massive bailouts by the federal government for the corporate sector is an example of Socialism for the rich, and illustrates that, despite claims of austerity, insecurity, and faith in the market, and in the midst of slashing budgets for the broader public, the United States has, time and again, determined that it indeed has the funds to do so. Think of the hundreds of billions to bail out the savings and loan industry in the 1980s; or the tens of billions for the airline industry in 2001; or the tens of billions for the auto industry, alongside the trillions that went to the banks and financial sector following the crash of 2008; or the tens of billions annually for farm subsidies, most of which goes to large agribusiness; or, of course, the hundreds of billions in COVID-19 stimulus funding already heading to the corporate sector, some of which was intended for small businesses, or was intended for the public sector but encumbered for outsourcing, as with the tech industry reaping funds meant to support public schools. There is a possibility of trillions more on its way with no transparency or accountability. Is the problem that there is no money for education—or an unwillingness to prioritize education?

FROM SURRENDER TO MOVEMENT BUILDING

Throughout this book, it has been argued that schools and universities have always served a sorting function, and have done that well. However, they have also always served as sites of ideological struggle, as one of the—if not *the*—central battleground for a society to define who it is and what it shall become. Not surprisingly, schools and universities around the world have also seeded revolutions.

In this moment, when there is so much reason for despair, I also see much reason for hope. Where I turn for inspiration and sustenance are social movements; the organizing and uprising of individuals and organizations and communities to collectively analyze, imagine, reframe, pause, redirect, instigate, illuminate—all in the service of changing society. Social movements change policy and law, they transform institutions and social relations and the very conditions of life, and they do so through collective action to queer the ideas that have become normalized and commonsensical, even among Progressives, including the ideas about the purposes of education, its problems, and the possibilities that lie ahead.

In just the last few years, teachers have collectivized, even when the law was against them, to shut down schools and rally their communities to demand more investment in public education, as well as to push their unions to be more Progressive, or simply to take over their unions altogether. Parents, alongside teachers, have collectivized to opt out of the onslaught of testing; to push out failed superintendents; and even a few years ago in Chicago, to stop the then-mayor from implementing his proposal to lengthen the school day without any change in what would happen—or any support for what would happen—during that longer day. Students have collectivized to lobby for safer schools and gun control, as well as to protest for swifter and bolder Congressional and corporate action to stop the destruction of the climate and the planet. Communities have collectivized to demand that Black Lives Matter, that the state end policing and incarceration as means of terror, oppression, and genocide, including in schools, where funding should instead be invested in services and resources for racial justice and community wellness.

A social movement is not the same as an event or an initiative or a campaign or an organization or even a network; it is not top-down, unified, contained, or the work of one person; and while it does aim to change laws and policies and who occupies leadership positions, such changes are not its only, or even its primary, goal. No, a social movement is of the masses; it is ground-up, diverse, fractured, and contested; and its most significant intervention is the changing of public consciousness, of norms, of common sense to see and feel hope that a different world is possible, and that each of us has a role to play in imagining and building toward that. A social movement can aim to drive society even more deeply toward Totalitarianism, or Fascism, or apartheid, or Colonialism, just as a social movement can aim to dismantle their legacies.

Historical narratives often focus on the role of leaders in changing society, such as the U.S. presidents in office at times of significant social transformation who get credited with corresponding changes in law or policy, like Abraham Lincoln and emancipation, Franklin Roosevelt and the New Deal, Lyndon Johnson and civil rights legislation, and Ronald Reagan and trickle-down economics. But none of these leaders acted in a vacuum. Lincoln was not initially for emancipation and ending slavery, as apparent when comparing his first inaugural address with his second, but he was pushed in that direction by Abolitionism. Roosevelt was able to gain Congressional support because alongside him at the time were vibrant organized labor and Left Populist movements calling for what would become New Deal legislation and initiatives. Johnson once told Dr. Martin Luther King, Jr., that he might agree that civil rights legislation was needed, but that the masses, the movement, was needed to provide the mandate to pass and enact controversial legislation. Reagan did not usher in the Conservative revolution—he was elected because of it.

Today, many of the signature actions by the Trump administration—implementing egregious tax cuts for the wealthy, building a southern border wall, banning immigration from several majority-Muslim countries—could not have been possible were there not vibrant social movements to inform, shape, resonate with, and propel them forward. Supporting Trump, and pushing the Republican Party to toe the line, are a wide range of movements and groups, be they Far Right and Alt-Right, White Nationalist and White supremacist, Conservative and neo-Conservative, neo-Nazi and Fascist, or Neoliberal and Corporatocratic.

What are the visions around which Progressives should be building movements today? Almost a century ago, the Liberal movements to empower workers of the industrial sector through the formation of unions, via the organized labor movement, and to advance redistributive economic policies and reign in corporate greed, via the Left Populist movement, helped not only to elect and re-elect Roosevelt as president, but also to provide the popular mandate for the New Deal. The New Deal was a set of social programs, public-works projects, and financial-sector reforms from 1933 to 1939 that would thrust the federal government into a far more hands-on role in regulating the economy and improving social welfare, investing significantly in providing immediate relief as well as long-term reform that aimed to address the underlying structural causes of the Great Depression. The New Deal was far from perfect, particularly in its disparate impact and neglect of people of color, as well as some women, such as women domestic workers. But even with its limitations, it improved the livelihood—employment, assets, prospects—for large swaths of the masses at a scale like at no other time in U.S. history.

The central lever of the New Deal was what critics would view as akin to Socialism—it was a set of public programs, run and funded by the government, that funneled funds and other resources directly to the masses via financial relief, direct employment, and social services, as well as public works that would benefit both rich and poor, such as energy, transportation, and other infrastructural projects. The logic of the New Deal was intersectional and systemic, premised on the idea that financial livelihood—income, wealth—was not only dependent on employment, but interconnected with a range of other institutions and arenas—healthcare, community wellness, family wellness, criminal justice, education—and therefore, that New Deal initiatives needed to include programs and policies to improve those arenas as well. This is why so many were lifted out of poverty so quickly. The New Deal is what set the precedent for so-called social welfare policies that would expand during the post–World War II and civil rights eras, particularly with an eye toward inclusion of different groups, namely, people of color and women.

Not surprisingly, this intersectional, systemic framing is what critics would be working to undo from the time of its inception. By the 1980s, the Conservative revolution had ushered in enough of a shift in consciousness to prevent any public uprising against the reversal of the New Deal–era bottom-up economics that would be replaced by the top-down Reaganomics, which would funnel money, tax breaks, incentives, and rewards to the top, purportedly so that financial benefits and wealth would "trickle down" to the masses. By design, trickledown reforms did not distribute wealth, and instead, the wealth gap grew and grew, to a point today where the wealth gap is greater than it was just prior to the Great Depression, as apparent in the unprecedented levels of concentrated wealth at the top and rampant poverty and un- or under-employment among the masses. Twelve years ago, following the subprime-mortgage crisis, this rhetoric of wealth trickling down once again reverberated soundly when the federal government spent trillions to bail out the banks and financial institutions that caused the crisis, lining the pockets of the banking and corporate elite, but with little subsequent impact on the masses that suffered the most in lost homes and savings.

Today, the logic behind the New Deal is making a comeback, thanks to the social movements to address climate destruction; like its namesake, the Green New Deal treats corporate greed and irresponsibility—and the economic policies and structures that enable profiteering at the expense of the natural world—as drivers of climate destruction, calling on the federal government to play an active role in addressing this crisis through legislation and initiatives. The Green New Deal examines the problem intersectionally and systemically in order to understand how saving the planet is inseparable from addressing destructive factors—from the failure of the economy and the legal system to protect the planet to the impact of war, conflict, displacement, and migration on natural resources—as well as protective factors—from just transitions for those employed in destructive industries to increased justice in food production and access, healthcare, and community wellness.

An Education New Deal would similarly name the primary forces that shaped the U.S. education system into the instrument of Imperialism,

White supremacy, and Neoliberalism that it was and is. It would profoundly increase the national investment in education, not subsidizing those at the top—through policies and programs such as incentives for corporate reformers and vouchers for elite private schools—but by federalizing funding and funneling it directly to the schools that serve the masses, with significantly larger budgets for everything from better facilities and supplies to better compensation for teachers and other personnel to better resources for support services, activities, and family and community connections. It would look intersectionally, systemically, and historically to understand how transforming education in order to function more in the service of democracy and justice entails not disciplining individuals, but working at the intersection of schools with the economy, the legal, medical, educational testing, banking, housing, war, and immigration industries, as well as community and social services, the natural environment, science and research, the arts—and it would emerge with a social movement that changes policy as it aims even more broadly to reframe how society thinks about the very purposes of public education.

Education must refuse its origins as an Imperialist, colonizing project. It must dive deeply into its central paradox of, on the one hand, aiming to be the "great equalizer" that Mann spoke of, even though, on the other hand, it was designed to sort and has done so throughout history, albeit in varying ways, with much force and efficacy. It must, in other words, constantly undo itself, remake itself, abolish the very conditions that made and that continue to make it the American project that it is.

When activists today call for prison abolition, they are not merely calling to close prisons. No, they are calling to change the many intersecting conditions of society that make prisons seem like the solution. Prisons in the United States have everything to do with White Supremacy, the legacies of slavery and Jim Crow, apartheid, criminal justice as a racial project, education as a racial project, the prison–industrial complex as a Capitalist project, the cycles of poverty, the fracturing of families and communities, the erasure of reasons for hope. Prisons, in other words, are American in all the ways described at the beginning of this book. And so is education.

What would it mean, then, to abolish the conditions that make schools and universities as they currently exist and operate seem like the solution? What would it mean to create the conditions of society that demand that schools serve not to conform and sort, but to democratize? What would it mean for schools to prepare students not merely to succeed in the world as it is, but also to imagine and create the world as it could be? What would it mean to nationalize education, to treat education as a collective investment and responsibility, as a public good?

What would it mean for universities to serve a similar function, not as a commodity to purchase, and not as a gift for the chosen few, but as a collaborator with communities and families to make the world a better place? What would it mean for education to tackle head-on the legacies of injustice that define its very origins?

Education as abolition?

An Education New Deal?

What would it mean to build social movements toward such visions?

Let's do this together!

About the Author

Kevin K. Kumashiro, Ph.D., is an internationally recognized expert on educational policy, school reform, teacher preparation, and educational equity and social justice, with a wide-ranging list of accomplishments and awards as a scholar, educator, leader, and advocate. He is the former Dean of the School of Education at the University of San Francisco, and is the award-winning author or editor of ten books, including *Against Common Sense: Teaching and Learning toward Social Justice* and *Bad Teacher!: How Blaming Teachers Distorts the Bigger Picture*. His recent awards include the 2016 Social Justice in Education Award from the American Educational Research Association and an honorary Doctor of Humane Letters. https://www.kevinkumashiro.com.